CW01468450

*Between Hell
and Charing Cross*

Between Hell
and
Charing Cross

Pamela Wilcox

London
GEORGE ALLEN & UNWIN LTD
Ruskin House   Museum Street

First published in 1977

This book is copyright under the Berne Convention. All
rights are reserved. Apart from any fair dealing for the
purpose of private study, research, criticism or review, as
permitted under the Copyright Act, 1956, no part of
this publication may be reproduced, stored in a retrieval
system, or transmitted, in any form or by any means,
electronic, electrical, chemical, mechanical, optical,
photocopying, recording or otherwise, without the prior
permission of the copyright owner. Enquiries should be
addressed to the publishers.

© Pamela Wilcox, 1977

ISBN 0 04 920051 8

*For personal reasons the names of people and places
have in some instances been changed. Limbo Hall is a
composite picture drawn from the author's experiences
in many London hostels.*

Printed in Great Britain
in 11 on 12 point Baskerville
by Clarke, Doble & Brendon Ltd,
Plymouth

For my father, with love

Contents

Chapter I

'Where is Victoria?'

They told me, Heraclitus,
They told me you were dead.
They brought me bitter news to hear,
And bitter tears to shed.

William Johnson Cory

'Where is Victoria?'

I don't know how many times during the last hour I had asked myself the same question. But still I had not got the answer.

Big Ben began striking midnight. I heard the echoing notes of the clock at Lambeth Palace, mingled with the distant chimes of the City churches, drifting down the Thames like a melancholy requiem in the darkness :

> But all the clocks in the City
> Began to whirr and chime :
> O let not Time deceive you,
> You cannot conquer Time . . .

I can never recall those lines without hearing the voice of the person who first read them to me. But for the moment I could not bear to think of his name, although his face had looked up at me all day from the obituary column of the *Telegraph*.

For better or worse, I have never believed in tomorrow. As a child, I hated that favourite adult expression 'You can always come back another time.' Whether applied to a visit to the circus, a butterfly chase across the Sussex Downs or the last day of the seaside holidays, that cheerful assurance invoked in me a sense of foreboding. Why should I have had such a precocious sense of mortality? Death remained a respectful stranger to my childhood, not even claiming a tame mouse or a favourite dog before its allotted span. Even during the war, almost alone among my contemporaries I lost no one close to me.

It was Robert, aware of the seemingly charmed life of my friends, who had warned me that each one of us has to live through his own personal autumn and the loneliness of watching the leaves fall from the tree of his own generation. This warning, coupled with my childhood foreboding, had ensured, or so I thought, that death would not find me unprepared.

But it did. Within a single year, with one very dear exception, I could say 'All my best friends are dead'. In sickness, filming in the Himalayas, boarding a train or dozing in a deck-chair, all were gone, the dear, not so old, familiar faces. The tree of my generation had been stripped bare. Today Robert was dead.

A cold gust of wind swept across the empty darkness of Parliament Square. I huddled closer to the side of the seat beneath the statue of Abraham Lincoln and tried to gather my thoughts. What had brought me here on this midnight pilgrimage? All I knew was that somewhere at the back of my mind this spot held the answer to the question on which my life seemed to depend: 'Where is Victoria?' The answer, if I found it, might be useless. But it remained my only point of reference and so I kept returning to it, and going beyond it to the even more frightening question: 'Why do I want to get to Victoria?'

It had started to rain, a soft fine spring rain. I lifted my face to the coldness, hoping it would help me gather my wits, throw me a lifeline. The word 'lifeline' reminded me of a routine test which astronauts undergo in preparation for the sensation of weightlessness. My name? I could remember all three of them. Professional, married and maiden. Address? The compass point began to waver. I lit a cigarette. Age last birthday? I could recall my last birthday party. There was only one other person present, the only other person I wanted to be present.

But I still did not want to think of his name. Just the same I did remember the song he made up for me and which we sang together :

> 'Forty-one today ! Forty-one today !
> I've got the key of the door,
> Never been forty-one before !'

The key of the door? I was automatically fumbling in my handbag for my keys. I found them, but could not think of any door they would unlock. I was trying to identify them when I found myself staring into a light, which dazzled my eyes so I could not see the face behind it.

'I've been watching you. Time you moved on.'

Like a rabbit caught in the headlamps of a car, I was still staring into the light. I knew subconsciously that the voice behind it belonged to a policeman.

'You heard me. Move on !'

I must have looked bewildered because the voice suddenly became kinder.

'Lost ?'

'I seem to have lost my sense of direction.'

There was a sound like a laugh. 'Westminster's a bit off your beat. On the game, I suppose ?'

I blinked in the light and repeated 'On the game ?'

I was now talking to a face and not a lamp.

'First time in London ?'

'No, I've lived here most of my life.'

'Trying to be funny, eh !'

'I'm not trying to be funny. I simply can't remember. Where is Victoria ?'

'Victoria? Well, now let me see. Carry straight on over Westminster Bridge till you get to the Elephant and Castle, then turn left.'

Elephant and Castle? Surely that was not the way to Victoria? Perhaps he thought I was just having him on about having lost my way?

'Step lively now. You can't miss it !'

The authority in his voice reassured me. I got to my feet.

'Thank you, Officer.'

But he had turned and was already walking away. I stood for a moment thinking over his directions.

'You heard me now. I don't want to tell you again!' The policeman had stopped and was calling to me over his shoulder. 'Let's see you get moving!'

As soon as I had reached the other side of the Thames I began to have doubts. But it was not until half an hour later that the character of the streets, the colour of the buildings, the very air, seemed unfamiliar, even alien. Perhaps I had not turned left soon enough?

Now lost in a maze of dark streets and derelict factory sites, I kept on walking, hoping I would come to a familiar landmark. For the first time I was beginning to feel physically as well as mentally tired, when I came out of a small dark turning and was dazzled as if by car headlights reflected off some convex tower. Doubting my vision, I decided to investigate and stepped off the kerb to cross the main road. A lorry almost took my toes off and caught the strap of my shoulder-bag, flinging it into the road. Another lorry followed, embedding my bag deeper into the tarmac.

At last the convoy passed. I stepped forward. There was a screech of brakes, the blast of a horn, then nothing.

I awoke after what seemed a long sleep to hear the jangling of an ambulance bell. I was lying in the road. A voice said 'No bones broken. Concussed, perhaps.' I was lifted on to a stretcher and found myself lying inside a dimly lit vehicle.

'Where am I?' I asked.

'Elephant and Castle,' a voice replied. 'Take it easy.'

'I want to go to Victoria . . . the policeman said turn left.'

'That's right,' said the voice, pulling a scarlet blanket up to my chin. 'We've turned left.' Then again oblivion.

I felt myself being carried out. 'Is this Victoria?' I asked, although I really did not care any more.

'Guy's Hospital,' the voice said. 'Don't worry.'

I lapsed into unconsciousness again and awoke to hear more voices. 'She's all right. Nothing broken. Knock on the knee-cap, that's all.' 'Where does she live?' asked another voice. 'Anything in her bag to tell?' I saw my battered handbag being examined. Something dropped out. My pocket mirror, smashed to pieces.

'No. She should stay the night, but we haven't a bed in the hospital.'

I was now fully awake. They looked at me.

'Like some coffee?' asked the nurse.

I shook my head.

'What's your address?'

'I don't know. But I'll find the way. Once I get to Victoria,' I said, trying to get up.

'Shall we call a taxi?' asked the nurse.

'No, I'll walk. I need some air.'

'You need sleep, not air.'

'Shall I drop her at a hostel?' asked the ambulance driver.

'Yes, do that, Bert.'

I found myself once again sitting on a bed in the ambulance. I had ceased to care where we were going. We came to a halt. The ambulance had stopped in a dark, narrow street.

'Not much of a place,' said Bert, noticing my apprehension. 'But what you need is sleep. Take my advice, kip and skip.'

As he drove off, Bert called out 'Good luck. And give my regards to Bloody Mary.'

I looked up at the place where I was to spend what was left of the night. By the light of a match I found the door bell. Beneath it was the legend 'Females only'. I crossed my fingers and rang. After a long wait there was a rattle of bolts and chains. The door swung open and there she was.

'Have you a bed for the night?' I asked.

Bloody Mary did not reply. With a rattle of her key-ring, she beckoned me to follow her across a cold cell-like lobby to a makeshift reception desk. For a moment she appeared to be studying a battered register. Then, peering up at me through the thick, shining lenses of her glasses, she chuckled and said 'There's one at the top. There's always room for them that can pay. It's ten shillings a night. One pound in advance.'

I opened my purse, took out some coins and put them in the grubby outstretched palm.

'Thanks,' I said, 'but I'll only be staying one night.'

'I said one pound in advance. That's the rule of the house. Take it or leave it.'

Too weary to argue, I took out some more money and put it into her still-outstretched palm. Bloody Mary pocketed it, then reached for a bunch of small coloured discs hanging on a hook. She picked out a yellow one attached to a frayed cord.

'Put this on. And don't lose it.'

'What is it?' I asked.

'Your number.'

'Thank you.' I was about to slip it into my handbag, when she snatched it from my hand.

'You wear it round your neck. Oopla!' And with one swift gesture she slung the disc over my head.

'Follow me, Number Twenty-two,' she said, picking up an electric torch.

As I followed Bloody Mary's squat, deceptively homely figure up the stone stairway, little did I realise that I had embarked on a journey from which for so many there is no return. In the months that lay ahead, I was to wear other coloured discs, but that first metal disc was symbolic in colour. Yellow. Like the Star of David, the brand of a homeless race, that disc was to become my passport, entry visa and identity card in a world of lost identities.

The most lasting impression of my initiation into that world is not of any one face or incident, nor even of the view of human misery that awaited me at the top of the dark stairway. It is the rattle of Bloody Mary's keys.

With a flick of her key-laden wrist she signalled a halt on the stairway, and with another she motioned me to go on. On each landing she repeated the gesture until at last we reached the top. It took me by surprise. One minute I was facing a heavily-barred door, the next bolts were pulled back, a key grated in the lock and Bloody Mary's arm pushed me forcefully through the door into pitch darkness.

It was like stumbling through the entrance of an underground tomb. There was an odour of stale linen, dust and decay. A jangle of keys, the flick of a switch and the harsh glare of fluorescent lights illuminated a vast low-ceilinged attic occupied by rows of camp beds on which lay formless shapes shrouded by grey blankets.

In the first glare of the light I was reminded of Henry Moore's wartime lithograph 'Sleepers in the Underground'. But whereas Moore's sleeping figures were discernible human forms, fused in a frieze depicting humanity's courage in the face of death, what lay before me now possessed the sombre despair of a Hogarth etching.

'Your bed's at the end, under the skylight.'

Click. The lights went out. The heavy door slammed shut. The bolts jarred. The key grated in the lock again. In almost total darkness, I stood listening to the rattle of Bloody Mary's keys as she descended the stairs.

By the pale triangular glow of the skylight I groped my way down the narrow aisle separating the rows of beds. Some of the shapeless forms turned and moaned as I passed. At last I reached number twenty-two, a narrow camp bed, with less than three feet separating it from the identical beds on either side.

I had not realised how tired I was. Thankfully I sank down on the hard mattress. For a few minutes I sat there, clinging to the edge of the rickety bed, then gradually my eyes became accustomed to the gloom. The fitful rise and fall of laboured breathing was the only proof that within these windowless walls over eighty women were alive. Moving cautiously, I took off my raincoat and hung it over one of the struts at the foot of the bed. Off came my sweater, skirt, shoes and stockings. I stood shivering in my bra and pants. I pulled back the grey blankets and was about to dive between the sheets when suddenly I realised there were no sheets, nor pillows either. Too tired to care, I pulled the blankets up to my chin. A nauseating wave of carbolic knocked the breath out of me. The second sickening breath made me cough and retch.

'Shut yer bloody cake 'ole, carn't yer?'

The voice from the huddled shape on my left was so close it sounded as if it came from my own bed.

I comforted myself with the thought that no bed bugs could survive asphyxiation. In the morning I would slough off the stench with a hot bath and clean clothes. Then I remembered.

B

I had no change of clothes. Wearily, I flung back the stinking blankets, stripped off my bra and pants, then dived back into the carbolic tent.

Perhaps it was the feeling of suffocation that brought back a childhood memory of my first anaesthetic. The sensation of the chloroform mask clapped over my nose came flooding back, and the anaesthetist's voice telling me to count ten backwards. Taking a deep breath, I started counting. Nine, eight, seven. Seven? What was it that the Jesuits had told me? 'Give us a child at the age of seven and we will tell you what he will be when he is a man.'

I had been a child of seven when we moved to Hill-Top, at Elstree. 'Hill-Top, Elstree.' I repeated the familiar much-loved names under my breath. These had been the signposts that marked out my childhood world.

How close to me that world suddenly seemed. I found myself listening for my mother's voice calling us in to tea from the orchard. Lying wide-eyed in the darkness, I clearly heard my father's jubilant cry of 'Cowboys and Indians!'

I had been just seven when I first understood the meaning of that phrase. As I closed my eyes I waited once again to hear the sound of my father's voice.

Chapter 2

Cowboys and Indians

Now I was young and easy under the apple boughs,
About the lilting house and happy as the grass was green.
                                                    Dylan Thomas

'Well, here we go again,' exclaimed my father, raising his glass
of orange juice as if it were champagne. 'Cowboys and
Indians!'

'What your father means,' explained my mother, 'is that he
is going to start a new film today.'

'What's a film?' I asked with the blunt curiosity of a seven-
year-old.

'It's a story told in pictures,' answered my father.

'Does it have a happy ending?' inquired my five-year-old
brother.

'My pictures do!' said my father. It was a good summing
up of the philosophy of one who was to become one of the
leading film-makers of his time. 'Cowboys and Indians!' became a regular breakfast-time chant. It was typical of my
father that he should make his profession sound like an exciting
new game.

Film, in its most physical sense, had first come into our lives
two years earlier. We were living in a flat in Kensington and,
as it was nearing Christmas, my mother had taken us to Harrods to do some window-shopping. On returning home, she
went to switch on the lights. Nothing happened. Our electricity
had been cut off because of an unpaid account. Our father
was in the middle of the first gamble of his career. While completing his film *Chu Chin Chow,* he had run out of money

and was reduced to having to cut the film himself in a cubby-hole in Wardour Street. Finally, he couldn't even raise the rent on this haven. With the help of my mother our bathroom was converted into a cutting room and for a week my father completed the cutting of the film while we ran around with supplies of candles. And in those days film was highly inflammable.

Two days before Christmas my father held a viewing of the film. The exhibitors bought it on the spot. The lights came on again, and on Christmas Eve my father rushed into the doorway yelling:

'Come on! We're going to Harrods.' He turned to my puzzled mother. 'Buy the children anything they want and buy yourself a fur coat, too.'

Harrods was about to close when we arrived, but my father brushed the commissionaire aside with, I suspect, a ten-bob note in his palm and we had a jamboree in the toy department.

There is an ironic footnote to that memorable Christmas. Thinking we were broke, my mother had bought us all gifts from a pavement salesman. On Christmas day, when all the excitement of the unwrapping was over, it was not the expensive toys that we loved best but the tiny clockwork toys from the pavement salesman.

However, we never took our good fortune for granted. I remember one of the objects installed in our new Elstree home was a polar bear rug. I remember hugging its stuffed head and nicknaming it 'Rich'. Rich we suddenly were and I realised it with a child's perception. It was a realisation which went hand in hand with my sensing that my father was a gambler. I do not think in retrospect he would disagree with that description, for his subsequent career as an independent film-maker justified the gamble.

Years later, during my father's bankruptcy hearing, the great documentary film-maker John Grierson remarked to me 'Herbert Wilcox wasn't born in Cork for nothing. You see, he's unsinkable!'

He proved it by writing his way out of bankruptcy and he sold his autobiography, *Twenty-five Thousand Sunsets*, to two papers at once.

Owing to his mother's bad health, my father's family had

emigrated from Cork to England and eventually settled in Brighton. He vividly recalls the privations of those days in his autobiography. One day he lined up at a Brighton pie-house for a fourpenny pie. When he had finished, he asked for more. 'What's your name?' asked the proprietor. 'Oliver Twist?' 'No,' replied my father without the flicker of an eyelid. 'Herbert Wilcox.'

After doing a variety of jobs from selling newspapers to dancing in a chorus, my father joined the Royal Flying Corps. When the war was over, he returned to Brighton with nothing in his pocket but a £117 gratuity and no plans for the future. It was about this time he met my mother. She was a war widow, her husband having been killed in action in 1915. She was a member of the Carl Rosa Opera Company. 'We often entertained in the officers' mess,' my father writes, 'and she used to sing excerpts from *The Maid of the Mountains*. She was also an artist – in short, a complete woman.'

I remember my mother as a glamorous person. She was not pretty, but had a beautiful figure and Dietrich-like legs. My father used to say jokingly that he had 'picked her up' on Brighton Pier. The truth is that he was among the audience one night when she was singing in a production of the Carl Rosa opera at the Pier Theatre. He was so taken with her voice and personality that he went round to the stage-door and waited for her to come out. Although he had only seen her that night, he introduced himself as an ardent fan. On the strength of this gambit, my mother found herself saying 'yes' to his invitation to supper. They were married a fortnight later at Brighton Registrar's office.

One day my father received a telephone call from his brother saying there was an opportunity for a film salesman in the Yorkshire area. He took the job. His first reaction to this new world was not very enthusiastic. Then he earned fifty pounds in his first week. He writes in his book :

'I certainly knew my Yorkshire before long, but it was tough-going, travelling from village to village on foot . . . I would sit in smelly, smoky, flea-pits, waiting for the boss . . . It was there in front of a flickering screen and the interminable piano accompaniments that I learnt much about audience taste and reaction.'

The two brothers were making a fair living, but typically my father was not content. 'If we can make this sort of money as salesmen,' he said to his brother, 'why don't we set up on our own?'

This was a bold suggestion. Owing to the war, the majority of films were made and distributed by Americans. There was no such thing as a British film industry. Nevertheless, with his gratuity and a loan of £500, my father set out to rectify the situation. Inspired by D. W. Griffith, whose film *Intolerance* he had not only distributed but had seen many times, my father set out to find a simple story that could be made within a small budget. This was *A Wonderful Story*. Ironically, for one to whom critics have not always been kind, it got wonderful notices but emptied the cinemas. But my father was offered £4000 to sell it outright, giving him roughly £2000 profit.

From producing and selling films the next logical step was to build his own studios. For his site he chose a Hertfordshire village and with our move to Hill-Top, a large rambling house at Elstree, my childhood really began.

Our father told us that when we passed a certain crossroads on the Mill Hill by-pass, we must all shout together 'Bang into the country!' And we did. And it was. We had never seen the country before. It was like being drunk with joy at the sounds and sights and smells.

Hill-Top lived up to its name. It stood in its own grounds, consisting of two paddocks, a delightful garden and a view of Hertfordshire's rolling, unspoiled countryside. The only mark on the landscape which we could see from our nursery windows was, symbolically enough, my father's newly built studios.

There were soon to be four children. I was the eldest, then came John, followed by Paddy (a girl who had been named after a film my father was making at the time, *Paddy the Next Best Thing*) and Sheila, the baby, who was born at Hill-Top.

With typical swiftness my father appointed the rest of the

household – our nanny, a nursery-maid, a governess, a cook, a butler, a general maid, two gardeners, two grooms to look after our growing number of horses, and two chauffeurs, one of whom drove my father's only grandiose personal acquisition, the Daimler.

A drive in the Daimler was a great treat for us, although I think our father got just as much delight out of it as we did. He bought it from the Crown Prince of Italy and it had a bonnet eight feet long. 'Sit in the back seat on a foggy day,' he told us exuberantly, 'and you can't see the front of the bonnet!'

Our greatest passion was our horses. My mother, an expert horsewoman, had taught us all to ride on a gentle, ancient cob. Eventually we all had ponies of our own and I became a veteran rider at local gymkhanas and horse shows. Hunting was a different story. I attended my first and last meet when I was eight years old. Accompanied by my groom, I was one of those who were in at the kill and, as the youngest member of the hunt present, the Master selected me for the signal honour of being 'blooded'. This ceremony requires the Master to sever the dead (one hoped) fox's tail and smear its blood over the new rider's cheek.

'Don't forget,' chuffed the Master as he anointed my small face, 'you mustn't wash this off. It's bad luck!'

My reply was to be violently sick over his boots. I shall always remember that ten-mile hack home with the dried blood burning on my cheeks. As soon as I got home I rushed to the bathroom and washed my face. Then I retired to my bedroom and locked the door. I felt I had behaved in a childish way and my parents would laugh at me. As it happened the sympathetic groom had told my mother the whole story. Foxhunting was never mentioned again in our household and I found the thrills of a drag-hunt were enough for me.

By now the pattern of our lives had settled down to a long country idyll. But it was an existence which had its own strict disciplines, for instance we were forbidden ever to go outside our own grounds unless accompanied by an adult. Visits to London were so few that it seemed as far away as Baghdad. Our governess was kind, but made us adhere strictly to the

timetable for our lessons. Apart from a yearly visit to the circus
we had no organised outings. I was nine before my father would
allow me (accompanied by my nurse) to see a film. It was
called *Seventh Heaven* and starred Janet Gaynor and Charles
Farrel. At about the same time we paid our first visit to the
studios, but there were no regular visits until I was in my
teens.

It was almost as if my father were saying 'Don't be in too
much of a hurry to meet the adult world, it will meet you soon
enough.' In fact, his world was already tapping at our nursery
door in the shape of the many celebrities he brought home
from the studios.

The first film star I remember was Dorothy Gish. She was
dressed in her tattered gutter-girl garb for the name part in
Nell Gwynn. With her red-gold hair dressed in ringlets, framing
a face like a flower, I thought she was the most beautiful person
I had ever seen in my life. Too beautiful to be real. This was
my invariable reaction to all the female stars I met. A rather
plain child, I often cried myself to sleep because I knew I
could never be a Mae Marsh or an Anna Sten.

The male stars were a different matter. Some of them turned
into adopted uncles. My father made a series of films based
on the famous Aldwych farces and Tom Walls and Ralph
Lynn were among our favourite visitors. Ralph Lynn was as
funny off-screen as he was on, and used to have us in fits of
laughter with his own version of leap-frog. As for Tom Walls,
that robust, debonair, horse-loving character became the object
of a secret crush on my part. And when his horse April the
Fifth won the Derby, the summit of my happiness was reached
when he allowed me to ride it on Selsey sands, where my father
had taken a bungalow for the summer holidays next door to
the Walls.

But the peak of my delight was meeting Ben Travers, the
author of the Aldwych farces.

At a very early age I became addicted to poetry. My godmother sent me a copy of *The Oxford Book of English Verse*
for my birthday. My mother thought I was too young for it,
but once I had read Matthew Arnold's 'Dover Beach' I was
hooked for life.

I started writing poems myself, all of them childishly deriva-
tive. I was secretly ashamed of my efforts and locked them
away. Then one day my father caught me with a newly written
poem.

'This is something I've always wanted to do,' he said, 'but
I have never had the time. Just remember kiddo, with a pencil,
a blank piece of paper and lots of imagination, you're queen
of your own world. Keep at it!'

He went on to prove his enthusiasm by having a book of
my poems printed, and one day he said to me at breakfast
'I've shown your poems to Ben Travers. I'm bringing him home
to lunch today. I want you to hear for yourself what he has
to say.'

I was so numbed with shyness at the thought of a famous
author reading my poems that I could not be persuaded to
join them at lunch. Instead I sat alone miserably in the nursery. Suddenly there was a knock at the door. It opened and
a stocky man with piercing blue eyes stood smiling at me. He
held out his hand.

'My name is Ben Travers. I couldn't miss the chance of
meeting a fellow author.' He held up my little book of poems.
'What do you do child? Wake up and dream? Well, just go
on doing it. That's how writers are made.'

By far the most memorable visitor was Sybil Thorndike.
She was playing Nurse Edith Cavell in my father's film *Dawn*.
At our first meeting she was wearing the make-up and costume
of Nurse Cavell. Indeed, we never met her dressed any other
way. Perhaps that is why we called her 'Aunt Edith' rather
than 'Aunt Sybil'. One incident makes it clear what made her
so instantly lovable to three young children.

It started one day with the invasion of our paddock by
workmen from the studios. What they were doing we were
not told and our father was obviously determined we should
not find out for he put the paddock out of bounds for twenty-
four hours.

The next morning he brought several of the film crew home
to breakfast. During breakfast I remember my father turning
to his cameraman and saying quite distinctly 'If it's fine, we'll
shoot Aunt Edith this afternoon.' (He now called her Aunt

Edith, too.) To my seven-year-old ears the word 'shoot' meant nothing in its film sense. In connection with Aunt Edith it filled me with foreboding.

'What does "shoot" mean?' I asked.

'Bang! Bang! You're dead,' broke in my brother, aiming an imaginary pistol at my head.

'It's only a film,' my father reassured me. 'You know, "Cowboys and Indians".'

But there was a cold, tight feeling in my chest which only increased when we were told that Aunt Edith would not be paying her customary visit to the nursery.

'What's more,' said my father, 'I'm putting you all on your honour to go to the playroom and stay there until I tell you to come out.'

I felt like crying and demanded in a strangled voice 'Where is Aunt Edith?'

'She's resting for the shooting this afternoon,' answered my father.

After lunch, with heavy hearts, we dutifully retired to our attic playroom. Then we realised why we were there. There was no window giving a view of the paddock, only a skylight which meant we had to stand on a chair to see out. Certain that something terrible was going to happen to Aunt Edith, we had to find out the truth for ourselves.

John had the first peep. Standing on tiptoe on the chair he called out 'There are some soldiers, and some men digging something.'

It was my turn to look next.

'They're digging a grave,' I said. Then I saw Aunt Edith. She was dressed as usual in her nurse's uniform, her arms tied tight behind her back. Facing her was a row of soldiers, their rifles raised and pointing directly at her. It was a distant view but somehow the distance lent it a terrible reality. Then I saw my father. He was waving his hand in the direction of the soldiers. The next second the small figure of Aunt Edith toppled over and fell to the ground. I shrieked and then John pulled me down from the chair.

'They've shot Aunt Edith!' I gasped.

'Don't be silly,' said John, 'it's only a film.'

At this moment our mother came in. She took one look at the chair and at our faces and guessed what we had been up to. What she didn't know was what I had seen.

When it was time for bed the three of us, tight-lipped and silent, retired to the night nursery. I was trying not to cry, but after our mother left my tears came in full flood and Paddy started to cry too. I was still crying when father came up to say goodnight to us. As he approached my bed, I stifled my sobs and turned my face to the wall, refusing to speak to him.

'What in heaven's name is the matter with you bunch of mugwumps?' demanded my father, appealing to John who was sitting up dry-eyed in the darkness.

'She thinks you've shot Aunt Edith,' replied John simply. 'We peeked. We saw it all, the shooting and everything.'

'Darlings, it was only a film. You know, "Cowboys and Indians".' But my father's pleas landed on deaf ears.

'I want Aunt Edith,' I moaned, my head buried in the pillow. Without another word my father left the room.

Many years later my father told me how Aunt Edith brought a happy ending to that day. Emotionally exhausted after playing the execution scene, she had driven back to the studio to take off her make-up and costume before returning to London. She was just leaving her dressing-room when my father's phone call came through. She listened to his story, then without a moment's hesitation said quietly 'Just give me half an hour, Herbert, to get back into my make-up and costume and I'll be there.'

'Why don't you come as you are?' he asked.

'Because,' she had replied, 'the children would never recognise me as I really am. If I turn up looking like someone else they may think I really am dead!'

All I remember is seeing that familiar figure framed in the doorway and leaping out of bed and hugging her with relief too deep for tears.

Years later when Sybil Thorndike was made a Dame, Sir Alec Guinness said of her 'If only everybody loved somebody as much as Sybil loves everybody, what a wonderful world it would be.'

But to me, she will always be Aunt Edith, who nearly forty

years ago ensured for three frightened children that over the green fields of their childhood death should have no dominion.

Inevitably we had to face school. The transition was precipitated abruptly by the departure of my parents on a six-month business visit to Hollywood. My brother John and I were duly dispatched to a nearby convent school.

The environment of the convent contrasted bleakly with home. My lasting recollection is of being plunged into a cold, gloomy establishment, where the rules decreed that we should be perpetually down on our knees in prayer. The nuns were kind enough but to the two of us, who had had no previous orthodox religious education, the emphasis on prayer and the life to come, with the possibility of hell and all its furies, was not even vaguely comprehended.

On my father's return, my brother and I pleaded not to be sent back the next term. Somewhat to our surprise he readily agreed. He added, typically, that anyway he had bigger and betters plans for us.

John was sent to Aldenham House, where he settled down to a happy uneventful school career which took him on to Mill Hill and eventually to Harrow.

My scholastic career was not destined to be so happy or uneventful. I started off as a day-girl at Radlett, a private school with a high reputation. My educational standards were up to par on most subjects, and thanks to our governess and my godmother I was ahead in English literature.

But unfortunately I did not get on with our English mistress. One day she asked me to write an essay on how an eskimo builds his igloo. Carried away by the subject, I wrote eight pages describing how I imagined the everyday lives of the igloo's inhabitants, a sort of eskimo version of *Mrs Dale's Diary*. My efforts were greeted with a couple of curt sentences written in the margin of my exercise book. The English mistress said she was giving me a low mark because I had gone outside my brief. She had asked for facts, not an overflow of imagination, and she underlined the word 'imagination'.

I must have been very upset because my father got to hear

about it and demanded to see what she had written. His reaction was volcanic. He picked up a pen and directly below the
English mistress's comment he inscribed a message saying that
he had no intention of keeping his children on at a school where
a penalty was put on imagination. Then he rang the headmistress and asked to see her together with the English mistress
first thing in the morning on a matter of urgency. I could hear
the puzzled headmistress protesting on the phone, but my father
was adamant. Then he put down the phone.

'This calls for champers,' he said grimly. (He always called
champagne 'champers'.) We were allowed a token sip. 'It's
goodbye to Radlett.'

Although we saw little of him except at breakfast, our father
directed our lives much as he directed his films. Sunday used
to be our favourite day, because it was the one day we had him
all to ourselves. We did not do anything more exciting than go
on long walks or watch the trains go by, but he used that time
to bring himself up to date with our problems. A few astute
questions, a word of praise for some particular accomplish-
ment, a rebuke which was nearly always disguised as a joke –
somehow he always seemed to set our small world to rights.
Above all, we liked him as a person. It is usual for children
to love their parents, but not so usual to like them as human
beings.

This is not to deny our mother's role. Her complete devotion
was without question and it was she who organised our daily
lives when our father was absent. For instance, we used to put
on a revue at Christmas time. Our mother sewed the costumes,
designed the scenery and soothed our rehearsal pangs. My
father thought our shows were good enough to invite many
famous people to them. One year we were even reviewed in the
Daily Mirror. It was our father who had brought us into the
limelight. But without my mother there would have been no
show. She was the life-giver, but he was a little larger than life
and had such a tremendous zest for it that we felt we were
being disloyal if we did not enjoy every minute of it as much
as he did.

Our days at Elstree ended as dramatically as any film.
My father's studios burned down. It must have been about

midnight when my father dashed into my room, his overcoat over his pyjamas.

'The studios are on fire,' he said quietly. 'I'm going down there. Help your mother to prepare for any pressmen that may arrive.'

I remember thinking that it was typical of my father that with his world going up in smoke he should think of the press. The worst might happen, but it would make a good story.

From the windows of our house we watched the flames rising high in the air. The wreaths of smoke drifting over our garden tasted bitter in our throats. To my amazement I found that tears were streaming down my face. At dawn we went to see the damage. The entire studios were gutted. As I gazed over the smoking ruins I realised that it was not merely a building that we had lost. Our days of 'Cowboys and Indians' were over.

Chapter 3

Marking Time

No war this year
    Daily Express, Summer 1939

The destruction of British and Dominion Studios meant that my father had to look for new premises to continue as an independent producer. Pinewood Film Studios in Denham, Buckinghamshire seemed the most obvious choice.

But other forces were influencing our lives, although it is only in retrospect that I realise our parents had drifted irrevocably apart. My mother's interests were her garden and the horses. My father was absorbed in film-making. But there were none of the quarrels or bickerings which can so often involve the children. It was accepted as a matter of course that my mother would often spend her evenings dancing at the Savoy with this or that partner. We felt no jealousy and when her attention seemed to be centred on the man she was later to marry, he was accepted as a good friend.

At that time Anna Neagle had appeared on the scene and was to change my father's life completely. Theirs was a most extraordinary first meeting. H. W. (as I now called him) was about to go into production of a film called *Goodnight Vienna* starring Jack Buchanan, but it had been held up because they could not find the right person to star opposite Jack. Appearing on the stage in *Stand up and Sing* at the time, Jack casually suggested to H. W. that he might like to drop into the theatre that night so they could continue their discussion about a leading lady after the show. The curtain fell on the first act and H. W. rushed back to Jack's dressing-room. 'Our search is over!' he shouted excitedly. 'I've just seen the ideal girl to star in our next film. She's your leading lady, Anna Neagle.'

H. W. was taking something of a gamble, for Anna's past experience amounted to only two years as one of C. B. Cochran's 'young ladies'. But it was a gamble that was to pay off. Anna was an instant box-office success, and so began one of the most successful partnerships in the history of British films.

When we first met her, we felt we had found a new friend. We recognised her extreme beauty and her glamour but were not overawed by it. In return she gave us a feeling of security, so much so that we saved up our joint pocket money to buy her a red setter puppy.

The answer to this seemingly puzzling matrimonial situation must have been in our parents' mutual agreement to postpone the actual divorce until we were old enough not to be too adversely affected by it. On looking back it reflects credit on all sides, and perhaps most of all on Anna, who was facing a situation which would have been intolerable to a woman of lesser character or understanding. The fact that she gave us children her genuine affection, while at the same time we presented an obstacle to her complete happiness, is something I will always remember with gratitude.

I was sixteen and completing what I hoped would be my final term at The Mount School, Mill Hill. In its day, The Mount had the highest reputation for advanced education, but my schooldays were not happy. However, I had many other distractions, notably the visits to my father's studios. My adoration had switched from the stars to the men behind the scenes. In particular, I was fascinated by the cameraman's job, and if I had been a man I would have chosen it as my profession. Luckily for me, my father's cameraman was Freddie Young, who has since become world-famous. He patiently answered my strings of questions, explaining the lighting angles and tutored my efforts with my own camera. I was enthralled by all the techniques and I determined that somehow I would be part of that world.

School not only separated me from filming and my growing library but also bored me. On balance, I agreed with Oscar

Wilde's remark that 'Nothing so retards education as going to
school.' So when my father came up with an alternative to a
finishing school I was cock-a-hoop. Paddy and I were to go
round the world, accompanied by a chaperone. He managed
to pick a New Zealand nurse who was old enough for the re-
sponsibilities, but young enough to join in our enthusiasm.

The itinerary was exciting : Marseilles, Naples, the Suez
Canal, Ceylon, Singapore, Hong Kong, China, Japan, San
Francisco and home across the American continent. We did
have fun, but what I had not realised when we started our
journey was that we were going to have a first-hand look at a
disintegrating world. It was a world which was dominated by
Kiplingesque characters, who still believed in the divine right
of 'the white man's burden'. It accepted as a matter of course
that there were 'haves' and 'have-nots'. Above all, it was a
world which was preparing for a long and dreadful war. The
first signal of alarm came when we were approaching Suez.
The papers were full of the Italian–Abyssinian war and rumour
ran through the ship that Mussolini was planning to blockade
the canal. Our fellow passengers, who were conventional British
tourists, with a smattering of colonial civil servants returning to
their outposts of Empire, dismissed the rumour as absolute
poppycock. Their smugness lessened when we saw the new
Italian gun emplacements near Aden.

Then in Ceylon there was the sight of half-naked children
diving for coins thrown by the passengers, most of whom
thought it was an amusing game. The sight of those squirming
bodies and their desperate little faces jarred my conscience.
Later, on taking a journey inland, I felt uncomfortable riding
in a rickshaw. The unquestionable servitude of the rickshaw-
boy's bent, perspiring back seemed so demeaning a way of
earning a living.

In Singapore, of course, we went to Raffles. There the chief
topic of conversation, over the iced gin and tonics, was the
destruction of the sea-front rock garden in order to put up gun
emplacements in case the Japanese should ever decide to invade.
'Nonsense,' huffed a red-faced colonial. 'The Japs would never
dare to invade while the British are here.' It happened that I
had just been reading *Inside Asia* by the historian John Gun-

ther, which predicted in minute detail just how such an invasion could happen. Gunther merely added that when they did attack, the Japs would come over the Malay Straits. Which was exactly what they did in 1943 and the British guns were helpless as they were all facing the wrong way.

China was the most pitiful revelation of all. We stayed at the Cathay Hotel in Shanghai which was owned by Sir Victor Sassoon. Stepping out from this palatial building we would pass, huddled in the gutter, a man dying from starvation without anyone taking the slightest notice of him. I saw much more, for instance the riverside slums in Tokyo, and the farmlands that lay inland from the beautiful shining city of Hong Kong, where children, their bellies swollen with hunger, were working alongside their parents like animals in the field. I vowed when I reached home to extend my reading to writers who knew and wrote about such social conditions.

On our journey from Manila to San Francisco we were scheduled to stop off at Hawaii, but a dock strike made it impossible. Our fellow passengers took the view that the strike was aimed at frustrating their enjoyment of the Hawaiian Isles.

We sat at the captain's table. His faded blue eyes took in every detail of his passengers' comfort. There was great consternation among the passengers because there was no ship's newspaper and even the radio was said not to be working. The captain brushed aside all their inquiries by blaming the situation on the strike. The result was we were twenty days at sea without communication with the outside world.

Eventually we docked at San Francisco and the first thing that caught our eye was a large news placard bearing the words 'Eddie quits'. We immediately bought a paper and discovered that our King had abdicated. Seeing our amazement, one of the ship's officers grinned and explained that the captain had not thought it fit that news of Edward VIII and Mrs Simpson should reach his passengers' ears and had therefore confiscated all the newspapers and jammed the radio.

Our train journey across America is my most exciting memory of the whole trip. The grandeur and variety of that great continent caught my imagination, and although we did

not put a foot out of the train, I promised myself that I would
return one day and explore it. Little did I dream that I was to
return twice and even make it my home.

We returned to England, and to a new house, Fulmer Gardens,
Denham, within two miles of Pinewood Studios. There were
obvious reasons why I never felt at home at Fulmer. H. W.
had moved to London and, above all, I had reached the age
when I wanted to be independent and earn my own
living.

My stepfather-to-be had built an enclosed riding school in
the grounds of Fulmer, and had started a Riding Academy.
So I drifted into helping in the stables, giving riding lessons,
and finally entering and passing the exam of the Institute of
The Horse.

I entered the *Daily Mail* Long Distance Competition, which
was a ride of a hundred miles, from Windsor to Eastbourne. I
had a good horse and came in second, which was not bad
going for a seventeen-year-old. But during the three-day ride
the experience of prolonged contact with the horsy set took
the edge off my enjoyment. I decided that they were not for
me. They lived and talked only horses and in particular I
found the girls very off-putting.

About this time I struck up a pen-friendship with the poet
Ralph Fox, who was later, alas, killed in the Spanish Civil War.
I was a great admirer of his poetry and had written to him, care
of his publishers, and enclosed a few of my own poems. To
my great surprise, he replied not from London but from
Madrid, where he was already fighting as a member of the
Spanish International Brigade.

I had been following the newspaper accounts of the Spanish
Civil War as I believed, in common with many of my generation, that this war was but a rehearsal for a world war. Fox's
letter struck fire in my imagination. I, too, would go to Spain
as a volunteer. I wrote to Fox of my plan, but he did everything
he could to dissuade me. Apart from anything else, he told me
that I would never get a visa from the Spanish embassy. This
was tantamount to a challenge and, unknown to either of my

parents, I travelled to London to visit the Spanish embassy. I planned to say that I wanted to travel to Spain to study Gitane dancing, but the Spanish passport official took one look at my passport and shook his head. They could not possibly issue me a visa as I was under age and my parents' consent was needed.

I did not ask for their consent because I knew I would never get it. Instead, I wrote a long letter to H. W. explaining that I intended to get a job. I quoted an advertisement for an assistant in a hat shop. I explained that I would live in London and my wages would cover room and board.

H. W. immediately telephoned and invited me to dinner at his house in London. He understood my need for independence, but why should I start off with a dead-end job? My brother John was already living with him and attending the Royal Academy of Music. Why should I not join the household as a pupil of the Royal Academy of Dramatic Art?

I protested that I did not want to become an actress.

'You'll learn much more than acting at RADA,' he replied. 'There's stage management and direction, and what is more, they have the most marvellous library.'

It was the library that won me. I agreed to take the entrance exam, which, to my surprise, I passed with marks to spare. At the same time I started tap-dancing classes and singing lessons, so I had plenty of scope for my energies.

I am very grateful for my time at RADA. To begin with I was mixing with my own age group and was forced to overcome my acute shyness in public. It soon became obvious that I was no great actress. My failure can be summed up by an incident involving one of my teachers, Stella Campbell, who was the daughter of the famous Mrs Patrick Campbell.

She was formidable and gave instructions in a voice that would echo round any theatre. I begged her to give me a small part in the annual Christmas show when pupils give a public performance.

'I don't mind what it is,' I said. 'I'll even play the back end of a horse.'

Mrs Campbell laughed loudly. 'Pamela wants to play the rear end of a horse,' she explained in ringing tones to the rest of the class. 'I ask you! What on earth does she think she's been playing these past months?'

I laughed with her. She had made the point which was becoming clear to me. RADA now had nothing more to offer me and I told H. W. I had no intention of doing my second year. H. W. did not argue on this point, but he still clung to the idea of my becoming an actress and promptly offered me a bit-part as a lady-in-waiting in his forthcoming production of *Victoria the Great*, starring Anna as Victoria.

It was my first and last experience of appearing on what was for me the wrong side of the camera. Word soon got around that I was the producer's daughter and the reaction was that I was taking bread out of the mouths of other actresses. Their hostility was emphasised, ironically enough, by Anna's kindness. She did all she could to help me over my desperate nerves and her other 'ladies-in-waiting' were quick to notice this. In addition, I had struck up an immediate friendship with Anton Walbrook, who was playing Prince Albert. He was a most kind and sensitive man and had immediately realised that I was out of my element. He insisted that I sat next to him between shots and we had long discussions about the poetry of Goethe and Rilke.

During the lunch break I used to take my meals with the other extras in the general canteen and none of them would talk to me. These unhappy experiences were lightened by meeting Jane, a fellow extra who was also playing a lady-in-waiting. She was exceptionally beautiful and intelligent but suffered from nerves as badly as I did. We were brought together by this bond and became great friends. Robert, her fiancé, was a young film editor who was also working at Denham. We soon became an inseparable threesome.

Robert had a deep love of poetry and introduced me to the work of such poets as Auden, Isherwood and Eliot. In short, he took me under his wing and being ten years my senior he nicknamed me 'the fledgling', because he understood that I needed guidance which my separated parents could no longer give me.

Eventually, I became bridesmaid at their wedding just before the war. After the war, quite by chance, I was to meet

Robert again. It turned out to be the most fateful meeting of
my life.

When the air-raid sirens eventually sounded on that Sunday
morning in September 1939 when war was declared, I was
killing time at Kingsgate. At H. W.'s cabled suggestion I had
taken a fortnight off from what he regarded as a dead-end job
as a sales assistant at Harrods. The next morning I travelled
up to London and went straight to the London Headquarters
of the Women's Auxiliary Air Force. They were not accepting
volunteers. Next I tried the ATS, then the FANYs. The most
encouraging reply I got was that I should try again six months
later.

Seething with frustration I returned to my flat. A friend
phoned to ask if I would like to go to the local flicks that night.
They were showing a re-issue of Frank Capra's *Mr Deeds Goes
To Town*. With the main feature was a news film from an
American series called *The March of Time*. This series had had
quite a success before the war, but as it happened this was the
first time I had seen it. This particular film was called *The
Ramparts We Watch* and concerned America's preparedness
for war. But it also took a dramatic and sweeping look at the
forces of fascism which were threatening the world democracies.

I had entered the cinema with no clear idea of what I wanted
to do with my life. I emerged with my mind made up. I had
just seen a piece of film-making which was new to me. It combined writing and film-craft in terms of living history. This was
what I had been looking for. This was what I wanted to do.
But *The March of Time* had been made in America. Where
could I find its English equivalent?

A quick phone call next day to my father's cameraman,
Freddie Young, pointed me in the right direction.

'There's one man you have got to meet,' he told me. 'He
calls his films "documentaries" and describes them as "the
creative interpretation of reality". His name is John Grierson.'

I immediately sat down to write to Grierson. Later I was to
learn he never received my letter. He was in Canada at the
time and it must have been lost in the wartime mail. My meet-

ing with Grierson was postponed but when I did meet him he re-mapped my life. Two other important names came out of that visit to the cinema. The first was Frank Capra, whom I was to meet and work for six thousand miles away from home. The second was the director of *The March of Time* film, whom I was to meet on the other side of the world too and eventually to marry.

Chance is a strange factor in life. A thin thread of circumstances can dictate one's whole future. In my case an illness triggered off a whole pattern of events. I became suddenly and gravely ill. A major operation was necessary and only my youth and good health pulled me through. The doctor ordered me to take six months' absolute rest. At the same time he must have written to H. W., for he phoned from Hollywood and insisted that I should join him in California for six months to recuperate.

'But I can't leave England now,' I protested. 'There's a war on.'

'Only a phoney war,' he retorted. 'Anyway, what use are you at the moment to King and Country? Come out and join us and I promise you we'll bring you back in six months, fighting fit.'

Despite all H. W.'s reassurances, I still felt something of a traitor when I sailed out of Southampton on the *Queen Mary*. At that time, passenger liners sailing for America were dubbed 'rat ships', reserved for those who were lucky enough to have found an excuse to escape from wartime England. But nothing could dim the excitement of my first glimpse of the New York skyline. After blacked-out London, it was like sailing into a great precipice of light.

Hollywood, on the other hand, failed to make much impact on me. True, after wartime England it was like arriving in some fabulous Shangri-la and I had a view from my window of the Pacific Ocean on one side and the snow-capped mountains of Yosemite on the other. But I kept telling myself that California was only a place of convalescence, where I could build up my strength before returning to England. Ironically, the stronger I grew in body the more homesick I became. Even visits to RKO studios, where H. W. was filming *Irene*, increased my sense of unease about being an exile in a strange world of artificial peace. H. W. and Anna shared my feelings. Indeed, they planned to return home as soon as their film was completed.

But to me, young and above all strong and healthy again, the waiting seemed interminable. To make the time pass quicker I started to write again. I struck out into new territory with some short stories, mainly with war themes. Then I hit on a story which I realised might make a good subject for a film. I called it 'A Darkling Plain', using the quotation from Matthew Arnold's poem.

I asked H. W. to read it. He was astounded. He offered to buy it immediately as the subject of Anna's next film. It was eventually shot with great success in England, starring Anna, and released under the title *The Yellow Canary*. The plot was based on the Nazis' plan to repeat the First World War blowing-up of Halifax Harbour.

At last I had achieved financial independence and I could go back to England right away. H. W. recognised that, even if I was under age, it would be useless to try to stop me. He made only one stipulation. On my way home I was to stop off at Halifax in Canada and do the research that would be necessary before a film script could be prepared.

I agreed willingly, although I felt apprehensive about exactly how much co-operation I might get from the authorities in Halifax. With the Battle of the Atlantic at its height, Halifax would be under tight security and the investigations of a young Hollywood writer might not be welcomed.

Eventually, I decided to go to the British consulate for advice. The Consul-General was sympathetic. He agreed that such a film was in line with the war effort of the British film industry. But he pointed out that nobody could get permission to do research of this kind in Canada without the permission of one man. As Consul-General he offered to write me a letter of introduction explaining the purpose of my mission.

'But who is this man?' I asked.

'He is head of The National Film Board of Canada,' the Consul replied, 'and his name is John Grierson.'

Chapter 4

Grierson and Capra

For me, documentary film is the creative interpretation of reality.
John Grierson

If it hits you right off, it's good entertainment.
Frank Capra

My first meeting with Grierson was not in Ottawa but New York.

I had sent him a copy of my screenplay outline and a few of my short stories. Grierson had no time for letters. He cabled me a reply asking me to meet him in the bar of the Warwick Hotel on 55th Street. Now that I was going to meet him at last I was overcome with nerves. As I stood tentatively in the doorway of the bar, a slight man rushed forward to greet me. He grasped both my hands firmly in his. 'You're Pamela Wilcox,' he said. 'Has anyone ever told you that you write like a princess?' Still holding one of my hands as if I was some precious object which might escape him he led me to the bar, his words spilling out in a staccato torrent :

'You know you're wasted on this Hollywood stuff.' He indicated my film script. 'But your short stories are the real thing. What would you say to the idea of coming to work for me in Canada? I can only offer you peanuts by Hollywood standards, but I can make a film-maker out of you. Come to Ottawa and I'll prove it !'

I protested faintly that I wanted to return to England. Grierson was unperturbed. 'Give yourself three months at the

National Film Board, then I promise I'll send you to England.'

The sheer decisiveness of his approach took my breath away. Within five minutes of our meeting, he had offered me the chance I had been looking for.

'Well,' he said abruptly, 'what do you say, yes or no?'

I wanted to say that it was an offer which fulfilled my wildest dreams, but only managed to answer 'Yes'.

'Good,' he said. 'And now that's settled, what will you drink?'

'I don't drink,' I replied.

'Well just remember, if you ever start, don't drink more than half a bottle of whisky a day.'

I thought this was rather extraordinary advice to give an eighteen-year-old teetotaller. But then everything about him was extraordinary. He was already taking out his diary and asking me what date I could report to Ottawa. Only reluctantly did he agree that I first had to go to Halifax to fulfil my contract with H. W. He also offered to supply the necessary letters of introduction to the Halifax port authorities. Then he suggested I should delay my trip to Halifax for two weeks and stay in New York.

'Why New York?' I asked.

'Because,' he replied tersely, 'this is where your education begins. I shall show you New York.'

Besides being the inventor of the British-based documentary film, Grierson had spent a year as film critic on several famous American newspapers. For the next two weeks, with Grierson at my side as a voluble interpreter, I spent my mornings at the Museum of Modern Art, which had a library of all the great films of the world. I sat through everything from Eisenstein's *Battleship Potemkin* via the Marx Brothers, John Ford and Will Rogers to *Felix the Cat*. Afterwards Grierson would take me out to lunch and deliver a brilliant lecture on the foibles of this director or that artist. I learnt more about the history of film in a fortnight than I could have absorbed in years of study by myself.

But my education did not end with film. Every day brought new revelations of Grierson's diverse interests. He took me to a small nightclub off Washington Square where he said I would hear a young girl who 'sang like an angel'. The girl was the then unknown Lena Horne. The next night he took me to see a very different artist, Ethel Merman in *Madame Dubarry*. I was enchanted with the Merman magic but was amazed to hear Grierson telling me that it was his third visit to the show. 'Merman's the best timer in the business,' he said.

Next came the wonders of down-town New York and Harlem. Grierson sat cross-legged on the floor with tears in his eyes as he listened to the playing of Jack Teagarden or the singing of Bessie Smith. Another of his passions was dancing. When he learned that I had been trained as a ballroom dancer he was exuberant. I could teach him. But, alas, despite his sense of rhythm, he was a hopeless dancer, though this did not dim his enthusiasm.

Grierson could not sing either, but this did not interfere with his friendship with Cole Porter. The two men had a sort of mutual admiration society. One night Grierson took me to Porter's penthouse, where the songwriter entertained us by playing all his hits at a large white piano. Grierson knew all the lyrics by heart and joined in, singing completely off key but completely happy.

To his hotel room came such disparate visitors as Sam Goldwyn, Dean Acheson and Charlie Chaplin. I was present during all these meetings. It was part of my 'education'.

Amidst all this activity Grierson found time to run his Canadian empire, either by phone or by sending dictatorial cables. The combination of the dynamic Grierson and the electric climate of New York gave me a zest for life which has never quite deserted me.

The two weeks ended. Grierson was off to Ottawa and I took the plane for Halifax. 'Don't forget,' was Grierson's parting admonition, 'you can wrap up this Hollywood business in a week.'

Working eighteen hours a day I did just that and arrived in Ottawa on the appointed day. The first impact of Ottawa as a capital city was a negative one. At that time the state of public opinion in Canada had a schizophrenic quality. As a nation she was suffering from an overwhelming inferiority complex, particularly in regard to America, who was not yet in the war. It was this lack of national identity and pride that Grier-

son's Film Board set out to correct. It is now acknowledged
that he succeeded. Not only did his films portray the Canadian
war effort in terms which it deserved, Grierson also achieved
something more enduring – he used film to bolster the nation's
awareness of its 'heritage'.

Life at the Film Board was hectic. A twenty-hour day was
normal. From carrying film cans I graduated to the cutting-
rooms and the mysteries of the movieola. The technical side of
film-making terrified me, and I made many mistakes. One
failure drove me to tears. I had been assigned to edit a film
called *High over the Borders*. It was about bird migration,
with a built-in parable that there would be no borders in a
peacetime world. I worked long and fruitlessly. I would get
hold of a shot of, say, a blue-tit taking off from a branch and
join it to a shot of what was anything but a blue-tit in mid-
flight.

At last I confronted Grierson. 'What you need is an orni-
thologist to edit this film,' I protested angrily. 'Point taken,'
replied Grierson calmly. 'I'll hire one from the University to
help you out.'

Swiftly I learned from my mistakes and began to have con-
fidence in the technical side. When my three-month appren-
ticeship ended, I went to Grierson to remind him of his promise.

'All right,' he agreed, 'you can go back to England. I will
arrange for you to sail on a troopship. I shall also be sending
over a young cameraman who has never made a film before.
Between you I expect to see a film about what it is like to cross
the Atlantic in wartime.' He introduced me to a nineteen-
year-old Canadian sergeant, Michael Spencer. Spencer was
clearly as frightened of his first assignment as I was, but he
summed up our situation wryly. 'If Grierson told us to go and
climb Everest on stilts we'd have a go!'

Nevertheless, three days later, two apprehensive teenagers
climbed up the gang-plank of the troopship *Empress of Russia*.
We were still at anchor in Halifax harbour when we heard
over the radio an announcement from Lord Haw Haw that
our ship had been sunk off Cape Race. Not a happy omen,
particularly since I had a secret horror of drowning at sea.
Then, the astonishing thing happened just as the crew were

about to pull up the gang-plank, a familiar figure came into view, his black trilby set at the usual jaunty angle.

Grierson's motive for joining us, when he could have flown the Atlantic as a VIP, was probably his determination not to ask any member of his team to face dangers that he would not face himself. His first words were 'Don't count on me to help with your filming; there, you are on your own.' He was true to his word, but his presence was the catalyst needed to turn out a creditable little film.

We had an uneventful crossing, except that the *Empress of Russia* was showing her age, and in mid-Atlantic we lost our convoy. So, when ships of the Royal Navy came out to meet us, to escort us through the last two hundred perilous miles to home, a great cheer went up from the decks. And players of the Canadian Pipers' band paraded up and down the deck playing 'Over the Seas to Skye' as we entered the green little port of Greenock.

As soon as we reached London, Grierson set about introducing me to the 'documentary set' – Robert Flaherty, Paul Rotha, Basil Wright, the brilliant young Edgar Anstey (who was to discover John Schlesinger as a film director) and that great Brazilian film director Alberto Cavalcanti. All became my friends. It was Cavalcanti who affectionately dubbed me the 'daughter of documentary'.

Before flying back to Ottawa, Grierson gave me my brief. My assignment was twofold. I was to spend most of my time at the Ministry of Information viewing all the film that poured in from our Allies and also captured enemy film. It was so intensive a task of documentation that I was often found falling asleep in the projection theatre at midnight. But I discovered I had a photographic memory and could fulfil requests for material from Ottawa promptly. The other part of my work was to direct film to feed the Film Board's requirements. I directed filmed interviews with Quentin Reynolds, Ed Murrow, Lord Woolton and even Churchill.

There was not much time for anything but work. But Edgar Anstey persuaded me to become a member of the Free French Club. I spent many an evening crouched in the cellar during air-raids while Alan Rawsthorne strummed 'Ten Green Bottles' on the piano. The most remarkable person I met at the French Club was Dylan Thomas, a cherubic young Dylan who only sipped light ale. I knew and loved his poetry and was amazed when he proceeded to lecture me on what seemed for him a most uncharacteristic subject, namely women's rights. His tirade aroused little response from me. I had never felt my sex to be a handicap and told him so.

'You say your childhood wish was to be a cameraman,' he raged. 'Why shouldn't there be camerawomen?' It was a point to which I still have no answer.

I was just completing shooting my first full-length film on women at war when I received a cable from Grierson. The rushes were fine, but he wanted me to return to Canada to film some material from the Canadian angle. So, one dreary March day in 1941, I was sitting in a hotel in Southampton awaiting notification of sailing orders.

At this point the Battle of the Atlantic was at its height. I prayed that I would be assigned to a solid troopship with a strong convoy. What I got was a mere 8000-tonner, a battered old banana boat called the *Jamaica Producer*. Crammed into this frail-looking craft were sixteen other passengers, including an American newspaper man, an English missionary and an eighty-year-old woman who shared my cabin.

The crew was made up entirely of Lascar seamen. The one who attended our cabin could speak a little English. His first approach was at once touching and frightening. He told me that the first thing that would happen if we were hit was that the lights would go out. Many people got drowned because they could not find their way up on deck in the dark, so I should practise walking up from our cabin to the deck with my eyes shut.

For the first twenty-four hours out of Southampton the *Jamaica Producer* made a pretence of keeping up with the rest of the convoy, then she gave up. Standing on deck with the American newspaper man, watching the rest of the convoy disappear into the distance, I was overcome by a great feeling of loneliness.

'I guess it's going to be a long, hard haul on this old tub,' commented the American wryly. 'Let's hope the bar holds out!'

By the fourteenth day I had lost count of time. We were sailing through mountainous seas and filthy weather, punctuated twice a day by lifeboat drill in which only the ever-cheerful Lascar seamen participated with any enthusiasm. The rest of the passengers had sunk into a state of lethargy and fear.

Amid the general boredom one figure singled himself out for speculation. He was the English missionary, who used to spend his days, no matter how rough the sea, firmly ensconced in a deck-chair within sprinting distance of our only lifeboat. It was the American newspaper man who commented on the fact that the missionary was wearing a VIP lifebelt, unlike the rest of us who had to put up with the kind that were inclined to break your neck on impact with the water. Likewise it was the American who discovered that the missionary was nursing a revolver in his lap. And why? The American had the bland answer from the missionary's own lips. Namely, that it would be necessary to repel the Lascar seamen, who would surely make a dash for the lifeboat ahead of the passengers if we were hit.

'Jesus Priest!' said the American. 'If anything hits this tub we'll all be sharing a lifeboat with a gun-happy Padre!'

Neither of us voiced the thought that if a torpedo hit a ship of this size there would not be anyone left to share a lifeboat.

On the fifteenth day, the small bar ran dry. It did not worry me, I was still a teetotaller, but the American was gloomy. On the previous night the violent zigzagging of the ship had thrown him from his bunk. 'She was taking evasive action against subs,' he explained. 'At this rate we'll still be at sea come Christmas!'

On the eighteenth day we passed the wreckage of some torpedoed ships. The only sign of life was half a dozen cattle swimming among the scattered wreckage. The mournful cries of those doomed beasts seemed as unnerving as the cries of human beings. Perhaps that was what triggered off my hour of terror. I lay awake all night listening to the groaning of the ship as she zigzagged her way through the invisible danger of waiting subs. Next morning, as usual, my eighty-year-old companion was up before me and dressing calmly. But when it came to getting out of my bunk I found that I could not move

my legs. I felt deeply ashamed. I was afraid. What was para-
lysing my legs was fear. By an extreme effort of will, I managed
to climb down shakily from my bunk.

I went up on deck in search of the American. I felt I had
to share my fear with some other human being. When he'd
heard my story, the American put his arm round my shoulders.
'You're no more scared than yours truly,' he said. 'Come on,
I'll show you something you did not know about this little old
tub. Only discovered it myself yesterday. It made me feel better
than a shot of gin!'

He led me down to the bowels of the ship and to the base
of the mast. He pointed out a metal plaque. Its inscription
described how the *Jamaica Producer* had been attacked by a
Focke-Wulf off the Irish Coast. When the ammunition from
their one anti-aircraft gun had run out, the captain had so
manœuvred the vessel that her mast split the enemy aircraft
in two and brought it down in flames. For this feat of bravery
the captain and all the Lascar crew had been honoured by the
King with this plaque.

On the dawn of our twenty-fourth day at sea, we at last
sighted land. In order to avoid Cape Race, which was a hot-
bed of enemy subs, the *Jamaica Producer* had battled on past
Halifax down to Montreal.

I have never been so glad to see a harbour in all my life.

As soon as I had checked in at my hotel in Montreal I telephoned Grierson to notify him of my arrival. He asked me to
stay in Montreal instead of proceeding to Ottawa, and said he
would be flying in next day with a VIP who would contribute
to some urgent discussions about new plans for my future.

The next morning my phone rang at eight o'clock. It was
Grierson summoning me to report to his hotel room. I found
him hunched over a whisky and soda, deep in conversation with
a ruggedly handsome man whose face was vaguely familiar.
As soon as Grierson introduced me I remembered having met
him at a government party in Ottawa. His name was Lester
Pearson, then Canada's ambassador to Washington. Later he
was to become prime minister of Canada.

'Pearson is my ally in a little plot I've hatched up for you,' explained Grierson. 'When you hear what it is, I think you will consider it a great honour.' There was an unusual pleading note in his voice which made me apprehensive. This time, I thought, Grierson really is going to ask me to climb Everest on stilts.

Then Pearson began to talk. He spoke eloquently about the implications of America's entering the war as it affected the area of film propaganda. The most important figure on the American scene, he explained, was the famous director Frank Capra, who was heading the newly formed US Army Signal Photographic Unit which was based on the West Coast. The aim of Capra's unit was to make films to help the orientation of the American GI. Naturally, some of these films would concern Britain's war effort. At the moment Capra was known to be looking for a British film representative. Then Grierson came to the point. Both he and Lester Pearson had joined forces and written to Capra putting my name forward for the post. 'But I know my Capra,' Grierson went on. 'He takes no more notice of letters than I do. You must go out to Hollywood and see him in person.'

I was momentarily speechless with surprise and not a little indignant. I retorted firmly that I did not relish the prospect of spending the rest of the war in Hollywood.

'Let's say six months then,' suggested Pearson. He added gently 'You'd be doing us all a great service.'

I was still inwardly indignant. By bringing Pearson along Grierson had put his 'plot' beyond the range of a personal demand and he knew it. Before I had a chance to voice my doubts about the success of this project, Grierson was giving me my travelling orders. I was to fly out to New York that night and catch *The Super Chief* at Pennsylvania station the following morning. From his wallet he produced vouchers for my plane and train fare, plus expenses to keep me for one week in Hollywood. If I did not succeed in seeing Capra within that time, I was to return to Ottawa where my job awaited me.

As I boarded *The Super Chief* the next morning, my feelings were that of a shanghaied sailor. During the three-day train

D

journey doubts about my mission crowded in on me. For once, Grierson had asked too much.

When *The Super Chief* pulled into Pasadena Station, the seasonal torrential rains were in full spate. It seemed an ill omen. Bearing in mind the limited expenses that Grierson had given me, I booked into a seedy hotel in unfashionable downtown Los Angeles – a far cry from the Garden of Allah, where I had stayed on my previous visit.

The first thing I did was to phone Capra. A toffee-voiced secretary informed me that Colonel Capra was in Washington for the week. When I explained my wish for an interview the toffee voice turned icy. The colonel would have no time for appointments in the foreseeable future. I think it was the secretary that first put up my hackles. I was suddenly as determined as Grierson that somehow I would get to see the unapproachable Capra.

By the time the first week had run out, so had my cash. I could not cable to Grierson for more money, that was not in our agreement. So to extend my stay in Hollywood I got a job. Because of the work restriction permits for aliens, I signed up as a car-hop girl at a swank drive-in off Sunset Boulevard. I worked on the night shift, leaving my days free to tackle Capra. I had to wear a very short skirt and a frilly apron. The working drill was primitive. Six girls stood at the ready waiting for a customer to drive in. The first girl to call out 'Car in!' got the customer and the tip, which was her pay.

Every day I phoned Capra and got different versions of the brush-off. Yes, the colonel was back from Washington but he left civilian matters to her and she knew nothing of the advance letters from Grierson and Pearson. She as good as told me I was wasting my time. However, by sheer persistence, I did manage to make contact with another member of his unit, civilian writer Robert Heller. Heller sounded impressed with my qualifications and was kind enough to say he would use his influence to try and get me an appointment with the great man. But he warned me not to hold out too high hopes as Capra was so difficult to pin down.

By the end of the second week I still had no further word from Heller and was on the point of giving up. Then a miracle happened. It was the sort of million-to-one chance which could only happen in Hollywood. It was close to midnight when a large red coupé swung into the forecourt of the drive-in. For once I was the first to shout 'Car in!' Even though he was wearing the uniform of a US Army colonel, I recognised him at once. The man behind the wheel was Capra.

I remember staring at him dumbly as he ordered 'eggs over easy' or some other American dish. Timidly, I inquired what he really wanted. He spotted my accent at once. 'Well,' he said with a friendly grin. 'What's a little Limey doing so far from home?'

'Waiting to see you, Colonel Capra,' I blurted. And before he could stop me I told him the whole story. For a moment he stared at me in amazement, then he burst out laughing. 'Well, little Limey,' he said, 'such tenacity deserves its reward. Be at my office at ten o'clock tomorrow morning.'

Capra's HQ was based in the old Fox Studios. To its inmates it was known as 'Fort Film'. Capra rose to greet me as I entered. Above his desk was draped a huge American flag. His manner was impatient, his speech abrupt.

'Well,' he said, 'I've read all the guff about you. Grierson seems to think you are a whizz kid. The only thing that has me guessing is this. Just how would you fit into my outfit?'

Inwardly, I was quaking, but I said boldly 'I could be your British film representative.'

Capra stared at me for a moment, then he grinned. 'Just how old are you?' he asked.

'Eighteen,' I mumbled.

'Jesus!' he exclaimed. 'The Pentagon would accuse me of cradle-snatching!'

He got up and started pacing the floor of his office. 'Just let's suppose for a moment that I took you on. What exactly would you do for me?'

I gave him a brief résumé of my massive film viewing sessions at the Ministry of Information. For the first time he seemed to be impressed.

'You mean,' he said, 'if I want to get hold of a shot of a sea-gull flying left to right over London Bridge you could find it for me.'

I nodded.

'What about material on the Murmansk run?' he persisted. 'I'm doing a film about Russia at the moment and I'm desperate for material?'

I was able to reply with a detailed account of the latest film material to come out of Russia.

Capra stopped his pacing and stood facing me. 'Okay, little Limey, you're in!' he said.

Then he grinned. 'Jesus knows what Secretary Stimson will have to say when I tell him my British film representative is an eighteen-year-old Limey, and a woman at that!'

He shook my hand. 'Welcome to Fort Film!' he said.

I walked out of his office and headed straight for the nearest cable office where I sent off a cable to Grierson, which read :

YOU MAY ADDRESS ME AS THE BRITISH FILM REPRESENTATIVE OF THE US ARMY SIGNAL CORPS CARE OF COLONEL FRANK CAPRA.

I received his reply next morning :

GOOD GIRL. GOOD LUCK. GRIERSON.

Life at Fort Film was one long sixteen-hour day. As the expert on all things British I was in constant demand which meant working closely with people such as Anatole Litvak, John Huston, Carl Foreman (then only a buck sergeant) and Robert Flaherty, director of *Nanook of the North* and *Man of Aran*. Poor Flaherty was somewhat out of his element. The complete dreamer, he had no time for politics, even in war.

I worked most closely with Frank Capra and John Huston. They were completely different characters, but equally fascinating.

Capra was the most natural and perfect teacher of his craft. Much that I know about film-making I owe to him. His method was to let you edit a piece of film the wrong way, and then gently and deftly put it right. This method took patience and a real love of transmitting knowledge. Besides being a great director, his skill in editing was unsurpassed and by reversing the order of the most elementary shots he could work magic into a mundane film sequence.

As a man he was above all a self-confessed sentimentalist, as anyone who saw films like *Mr Deeds Goes to Town* or *You Can't Take it With You* would guess. He was born in Palermo and never forgot it. Sometimes he used to ask us back to his house in the evenings and there in the company of his charming wife and old friends we would listen for hours to Sicilian music on gramophone records. Capra never forgot the hostile film critic who once wrote that he never went to sleep at nights without first reading the death of Little Nell. 'On the contrary,' Capra explained to me, 'what the bastard doesn't know is that I don't have to read it, I know it already by heart.' Above all, Capra was one of that rare breed in Hollywood, a perfect gentleman.

John Huston would be the last to claim that he was anybody's gentleman. Bizarre and boisterous, he ploughed his own furrow and paid no more heed to the War Department strictures than he had to Hollywood. He gave the Pentagon no peace until they reluctantly gave him permission to go to the fighting zone and make a film instead of editing battle material in the shelter of Fort Film. He led a film team into the thick of the fighting on the Italian front. Totally regardless for his personal safety, he faced several rebellious cameramen who were more cautious. He came back to Hollywood with a hundred reels of film under his arm which he eventually edited down to a film called *Casino*. Up till this point Huston had refused to show a shot of the film to any of the anxious Washington officials. I was honoured, along with the American novelist John O'Hara, by being allowed to see a private preview. What we saw was a film so full of the pity and futility of war that its final message was to call for an immediate armistice. O'Hara's wry verdict was 'Well, John, I don't think this film will do much to push up your pips to those of a colonel.'

He was right. The Pentagon generalship was reportedly aghast at what they saw and ordered that the negative of the film should be kept under lock and key until the end of the war. So Huston's greatest wartime achievement was destined for oblivion. But Huston was undeterred. He later told me that from his Italian experience of total war came the inspiration to make his first post-war film, *The Red Badge of Courage*.

But my most memorable working experience at Fort Film came out of an unexpected order from Capra. 'I want you to give me your opinion of the script of a film I'm going to make about the Negro soldier,' he said bluntly.

'Why me?' I protested. 'I know nothing about the Negro problem.'

'That's exactly why I have picked you,' replied Capra. 'I can be sure you are without prejudice.'

He then introduced me to an American Negro actor who was to play a part in the film, whom I shall call R. P.

R. P. had not a trace of the 'race chip' on his shoulder. This was some achievement in the climate of American opinion at that time. For instance, there we were sitting through reels of film showing the American Negro fighting bravely on all the battle fronts of the world when only a week previously Paul Robeson had been banned by the Daughters of the American Revolution from singing on the steps of the Lincoln Memorial in Washington.

R. P. was a non-smoker and a teetotaller so during the weeks we were working together we went to the drugstore across from the studios for lunch-time sandwiches and a milk-shake. These visits did not go unnoticed by the burly studio guard, who was more than just a dyed-in-the-wool southerner; he was the most bigoted man I had ever met, always sounding off about 'the yellow-bellied chinks' or the 'lousy Limeys'. An American version of Alf Garnett, but wearing a uniform, toting a gun and, thanks to the flask of rye in his hip-pocket, hardly ever sober, which all proved a dangerous combination, as I was soon to discover.

One day, when R. P. and I were returning from the drug-store, the guard put a hand on my arm as we were going through the studio gates.

'I wanna word with you,' he said in a confidential tone, waving me into his cubby-hole with his revolver. 'You didn't ought to be seen eating in public with that nigger. Nice white gals don't act that way in America. I thought I ought to warn you seein' as how things may be different in England.'

'You bet things are different,' I retorted. 'We don't look at the colour of a man's skin before we eat with him.'

The guard broke in furiously, 'That damned nigger will only take advantage of you!'

'Any more of that talk,' I said, 'and I'll report you to Colonel Capra!'

From that day on, I got no 'good-morning' salute at the studio gate. Then one night a week later the eruption came. R. P. and I had been working late in the projection room. As it was nearing midnight, we decided to retire to my office to talk it over. I was just opening a bottle of Coca-Cola when suddenly the office door was flung open. The guard stood in the doorway. He was swaying tipsily and in his hand he held his revolver which he pointed shakily at R. P.

'Whadda you think this is,' he growled, 'a fucking night school? You nigga . . . Get your black ass out of here before I put a bullet up it!'

He lurched forward, pointing the gun within feet of R. P.'s head. R. P. sat as still as a rock.

'Put that gun down,' he said quietly.

The guard's answer was to wave the revolver menacingly. 'You heard me, Sambo! Get moving!'

R. P. got to his feet. 'Don't move, Pamela,' he said in the same level tone. I was too frightened to move a finger.

'Give me that gun,' said R. P., taking a step towards the wildly waving revolver.

In the next instant two things happened. A voice rasped from the doorway 'Put your hands up!' The guard whirled round and as he did so R. P. grabbed the revolver. The tall uniformed figure of an American duty officer was standing in the doorway.

'Just as well I was working late too,' he drawled. Then he turned to the prostrate figure of the guard who had collapsed in a chair weeping tears of drunken rage.

'Get on home now,' said the duty officer. 'In the morning, I shall personally see to it that you get your marching orders.'

I was shaking from head to foot, but R. P.'s only reaction was to turn to me with a grin.

'Sorry you had to be introduced to our race problem the hard way!' he said.

Chapter 5

Hollywood Sweet and Sour

Los Angeles is several soulless suburbs in search of a city.
Aldous Huxley

I had been at Fort Film for nearly a year when one day, during the lunch break, Carl Foreman entered the studio canteen followed by a tall lean stranger wearing dark glasses. Everyone looked at the stranger, not because he was the only one among us wearing civilian clothes, but because everyone, including myself, thought he was Gary Cooper.

Foreman came straight up to my table and introduced us.

'Meet Loring Richards, straight from *The March of Time* in New York. You two will be working together quite a bit, so I'll leave you to get acquainted.'

There was an awkward silence as we sat facing each other. I remember thinking 'He's as shy as Cooper, too.'

To break the silence I asked 'So you come from *The March of Time*? Did you ever have anything to do with a film called *The Ramparts We Watch*?'

'I produced and directed it. Why do you ask?'

I explained that seeing his film at seventeen had been the turning point of my life.

'You might say,' I concluded, 'that your film is the sole reason why I am sitting here today, six thousand miles away from home.'

Impulsively, he leaned over and took my hand.

'That fact alone makes it worthwhile having made it,' he said simply.

I remember making some light-hearted reply and thinking that this American was not so shy after all. But I think I knew then that it was love at first sight for both of us.

He took me out to dinner the next night and we exchanged life stories. He was the son of a Federal Court Judge. His godfather was Justice Hugo Black, Roosevelt's chief legal adviser. Loring had studied law at Harvard where he also developed his passions for writing and films. After graduation he could not settle down and went with the Grenfell Mission to the Arctic as a student medical assistant. On his return he still had not found his true direction when he applied for a job with the film division of the Henry Luce empire. He joined *The March of Time* staff as a film-writer in 1937 and within two years he was made a producer. *The Ramparts We Watch*, which had won a Hollywood Oscar, set the seal on his career as the most promising American documentary producer.

I remember asking him what had been his most memorable interview as a *March of Time* producer. He replied that it was what might be called a 'non-interview' and had happened while he was working as a probationary reporter on a Chicago newspaper. His first big chance came when his editor ordered him to go and interview the American poet and biographer Carl Sandburg, who had just finished half a lifetime's work on a massive biography of Abraham Lincoln.

Loring drove several hundred miles out to Sandburg's farm in Wisconsin. He had great difficulty in finding it and when he finally arrived at a rambling old farmhouse he thought he had come to the wrong place as there was no sign of life. Getting no answer when he rang the front door bell, he walked in through the open door and was making his way across a silent and empty hall when something stopped him in his tracks. What sounded like the bleating of sheep came from behind a door at the end of a corridor. Then he recalled hearing that one of Sandburg's eccentricities was keeping pet goats in the house. Following his nose he knocked at the door and, receiving no reply, opened it and walked into a low-ceilinged room full of goats. Two were sprawled on the settee. Others chewed the cud in front of the French windows. At the far end of the book-lined study he saw a white-haired old man sitting at a writing desk, his head bowed over his arms. He recognised the huddled figure as Sandburg. Loring said that he would never forget Sandburg's expression when the old man looked up at him. 'He looked like someone who was stunned by a great and recent shock,' Loring told me. The old man gazed at him silently for a moment. Then he said in a very low voice : 'You'll have to excuse me. I have just suffered a great bereavement. I can't give you an interview today.'

It was then that Loring noticed he was wearing a black tie. His immediate reaction was to suppose that he had arrived at the moment of a sudden death in the family.

Sandburg pointed a trembling hand at a pile of manuscript lying in front of him on the desk, then he said 'This is strictly off the record, but my dearest friend and constant companion of the past twenty-five years died not half an hour ago. You see, I have just written of the death of President Lincoln.'

Driving back to Chicago, Loring knew that although he had spent less than ten minutes in Sandburg's company he had more than a story, he had a scoop. But he had already made up his mind to keep faith with Sandburg's stricture that his words were 'strictly off the record'. He fobbed off his editor with the excuse that he had been unable to find Sandburg's farm. The editor was furious and fired him on the spot for incompetence.

Loring was now thirty-five, his ten-year-old marriage was ending and he was in the process of getting a Mexican divorce because he wanted to be free before his call-up, which was imminent. It was on our third evening together that he said 'Now I have a double reason for wanting to be free in a hurry. Will you marry me?'

He obtained a quick Mexican divorce, and five weeks later we drove to Arizona to be married. It was prophetic that even at that early stage I felt uneasy about the emotional climate of Hollywood. I wanted to be married in a place that had more sense of permanence. We arrived at Phœnix, a sleepy Arizona town, about midnight and had to knock up the Justice of the Peace, who happened to be a woman, to perform the ceremony. Taped organ music played in the background and our witness was a passing cowboy. It was all over in five minutes and I felt that my wish for a sense of lasting security had not been fulfilled. Neither of us could have guessed what complications our choice of Arizona would cause us. But then, who could have been expected to know that Hollywood was to become a town of terror?

We had no time for a honeymoon. Loring had received his call-up papers and true to his romantic character he had turned down the forces in favour of joining the merchant navy, where he thought he would experience a truly democratic relationship with his shipmates. It was only 1943 and there was no hope of a quick end to the war, so I was sick at heart as two days later I drove him to San Diego to join his first ship. Owing to the vagaries of war he was only able to get leave twice and each time he landed in New York, while I was stuck at Fort Film. It was to be two years before we saw each other again.

Working flat out at Fort Film was my only distraction. I had no heart for social life and when friends did persuade me to go to a party it only seemed to aggravate my separation from Loring and from the war itself.

The climate of isolation that existed in Hollywood did not help. The only world event that made any impact was the death of Roosevelt. It was noon when the news came through on the teletape at Fort Film. Everyone, from Capra down, stopped work. I found myself with Carlton Moss, a Negro scriptwriter working for Capra, walking aimlessly along Hollywood Boulevard. Everyone else seemed to be under the same sense of shock. Stunned groups of people were streaming out of shops and restaurants and standing silently on street corners reading the newspapers. All commercial radio went off the air until after the funeral. The networks relayed only classical music. At intervals the sad voice of Carl Sandburg could be heard reciting Walt Whitman's lament for the death of Lincoln:

'Captain, Oh! my Captain, the fearful journey's done!'

While I was walking with Moss, I suddenly heard him singing under his breath a sad and haunting melody, and as he repeated it for the second time I asked him what it was called. 'It's a Negro spiritual written at the time of Lincoln's death,' he explained, 'and it's called "Death, Ain't You Got No

Shame?" ' The next morning when I opened *The New York Times* and turned to the leader, the headline jumped out at me. It read 'Death, ain't you got no shame?'

Loring came home a week after VE day. We immediately set off for Palm Springs for a delayed honeymoon. Loring had been offered a job as a script-writer at Warner Brothers Studios. As for me, I had broken into radio writing and on the strength of my first script, which had won the Stephen Vincent Benet Award for the best original radio play of the year, I was signed up by Columbia Broadcasting System. We rented a large beach house in Santa Monica next door to the beach house that had belonged to Marion Davies and Randolph Hearst. There were eight bedrooms and a heated swimming pool, although the Pacific lapped at our back door. The house was decorated in the style of the twenties. It was all white and chromium. With its glass roof open wide to the rays of the Pacific sunlight, the house seemed built on air.

For the first two years we were idyllically happy. Yet even then I began to discern an alien presence which was as strong as another woman : the presence of Hollywood itself. I enjoyed the success Hollywood brought to both of us, particularly to Loring, who now had a healthy contract with Warner Brothers. But what I found missing was any kind of roots, intellectual or emotional. For instance, I yearned for the theatre, for concerts, for intellectual companionship. Loring, on the other hand, seemed to have become completely blinkered to any aspect of life outside the orbit of Hollywood success. I did not feel I was growing in any direction since leaving Capra. Writing thrillers for radio was no substitute for dealing with the realities of the world. Famous names were no match for the excitement I had felt learning my job in Ottawa among John Grierson's young cavaliers. Year seemed to follow year without even the relief of changing seasons.

I was not alone in feeling Hollywood's isolation. At one Hollywood party I discovered someone else who shared my feelings. This was Lionel Barrymore. I still did not drink and felt the usual odd woman out as the party reached its climax. Errol Flynn decided to give an extra fillip to the evening by organising a nude swimming party in the Pacific. I am not a prude and was devoted to Flynn when he was reasonably sober, but I did not feel like joining in and found myself alone with Barrymore. He must have noticed I was looking a little forlorn because he asked me what was the matter, apart from the fact that I was obviously playing the reluctant guest among a group of retarded children.

'That's just it,' I burst out. 'Hollywood strikes me that way. I feel like an adult intruder at one gigantic children's game. Am I wrong?'

Barrymore sat silently for a moment, turning his brandy glass in his hand, then he said 'No, you're not wrong. You're only too goddamned right. Your trouble is you're homesick for the company of adults. I know how you feel, I've been here for twenty years and I'm the loneliest man in town. You know how I comfort myself?'

I shook my head. In the distance we could hear the shrieks of the guests.

'I tell myself this,' said Barrymore slowly. 'Hollywood began as a ghost town, it will end as a ghost town.'

Prophetic words. Today Hollywood is indeed a ghost town. The back lots where John Ford's stage coach once rumbled and Gene Kelly danced in the rain are giant cemeteries. Hollywood is as dead as the Roman Empire it so often depicted.

But in 1948 few could have prophesied this, nor how quickly the end would come or in what strange manner. For my own part I thought of myself increasingly as a misfit, a wife inclined to be jealous of her husband's absorbing love affair with Scott Fitzgerald's 'Bitch-Goddess Success'. At the same time, I realised it was practically inevitable that sooner or later the 'Bitch Goddess' would assume the form of another woman.

One incident illustrates our differing points of view about the community in which we lived. It horrified me but Loring took it in his stride.

We usually went out for Sunday lunch to the Brown Derby in Beverley Hills. Sunday was my favourite day at the Derby, as it was the one day when one did not go there just to be seen. At weekends all fashionable Hollywood trekked out to Palm Springs or Catalina. We had stopped outside the Derby to buy the Sunday newspapers. To our surprise our usual newspaper-seller was not there. His place had been taken by a man with an old face, framed by a mane of long white hair. We noticed he took a long time to produce our change. But there was something else about him which made me look at him a second time.

'I'm sure I've seen that face somewhere before,' I said.

'Probably some old bit player who's past it,' replied Loring.

We were sitting reading our papers in the empty Derby and had forgotten all about him when suddenly he made an entrance through the swing doors. Even though stooped with age, he came striding in, a giant of a man, with a broad-brimmed black hat over his white hair. Under his shabby coat he was wearing a sort of safari suit with knickerbocker trousers.

His appearance acted on the Derby staff like an electric shock. A flurry of waiters rushed forward and took the shabby coat off with the tenderness of those waiting on a child. The manager greeted him in obvious delight with a series of bows. The old man was ushered to a table next to ours and sat down with the dignity of a prince. The wine waiter hurried forward wheeling an ice-bucket. A bottle of Veuve Cliquot was uncorked, poured, and tasted by the old man who nodded his approval. He seemed neither surprised nor unduly pleased by his welcome but accepted it as his due. He raised his glass to the smiling manager and, indicating the empty restaurant, said wryly 'To absent friends!'

Then, out of the corner of his eye, he must have seen us. I think we must have been holding hands, for he raised his glass in our direction. 'Bless you, my children!' he said. 'And may your happiness outlast anything this town has to offer you.'

It seemed so natural that he should know we were in love and wish us happiness. Suddenly we both knew we were in the presence of a great man.

There was no further exchange between us, but there was a magnetism about him. We could not help watching him as he went from caviar to brandy and a final cigar. Then, at a wave of his hand, the manager appeared with his bill and a pencil. With a flourish, the old man signed the bill. The shabby overcoat was put on gently. Then, raising his broad-brimmed hat to us, he turned and was gone. No money had changed hands.

It was the manager who told us his story. The old man was

D. W. Griffith, the director of *Birth of a Nation*. D. W. used
to eat regularly at the Derby even after his career faded. Gradually, he came less and less often and finally he disappeared from
sight and from memory. Then one day the manager spotted
him selling newspapers and insisted he come in for a meal.
D. W. ordered a plate of soup. The manager was outraged.
How could an old client insult his cuisine so? With a smile
D. W. produced half a dollar from his pocket.

'That, my friend,' he said, 'is the present limit of my finances.'

'Mr Griffith,' the manager replied, 'you have always signed
at the Derby. So long as I am manager I hope you will go on
honouring us with your signature.'

'What about paying the bill?' asked D. W. quizzically.

'I have had the honour of serving you for twenty-five years,'
replied the manager. 'I can wait.'

The manager said he believed that D. W. only accepted the
offer because he was literally starving. So the ritual began.
But D. W. came only on Sundays. 'I wouldn't want to embarrass you,' he told the manager, 'by appearing when you have a
full house.'

We had witnessed the last Sunday lunch. Within two weeks
D. W. Griffith was dead. The event occupied two lines in *The
Hollywood Reporter*. But that fine character actor Eric Von
Stroheim was not too embarrassed to admit he was near to tears
that night when he went on the air to announce Griffith's death
to the nation:

'D. W. Griffith, penniless and alone, died here today. He
died in the heart of Hollywood. That is to say, he died in the
heart of the most heartless city in the world. . . .'

In retrospect it is surprising that five years passed before the
'other woman' appeared. Loring told me about her from the
start. She was a powerful executive in the Screen Writers Guild,
born and bred to Hollywood.

Loring was stubbornly practical about how he planned to
handle the situation. There was no question of divorce. At
least, not yet. For the time being Loring and I were to continue
to live under the same roof.

'We may as well be civilised about this,' Loring said. By now he even talked like a film script. But then my reaction was also predictable. I promptly moved out and went to stay with Judith Wilder, the estranged wife of director Billy Wilder. I supposed that eventually Loring would ask me for a divorce. At the time I told myself that pride stopped me from fighting for my marriage. The truth was that, although I still loved Loring, I was not sure I was in love with the idea of being married to him any more.

Then, something happened to Hollywood which made our own particular eternal triangle seem relatively unimportant. Senator Joe McCarthy announced that he was about to descend on the town. The so-called Un-American Trials that followed and which resulted in the imprisonment of the famous 'Hollywood Ten' received world-wide publicity.

The political manœuvres of the McCarthy machine have been reported so fully that any comment at this date is superfluous. But what is not so well known is the scale of the small tragedies that lay behind the headlines. What cannot be imagined accurately is the terror that engulfed the whole community. At the time, many people abroad wondered why McCarthy chose Hollywood as his chief target. The answer is simple. Hollywood was a community that had, even in good times, always lived on the edge of its nerves. It only needed someone like McCarthy to exploit the atmosphere for hysteria to be let loose. Under the guise of hunting Communism, McCarthy made every man, woman and child in Hollywood afraid of his own shadow. Nobody was safe. People otherwise sane jostled each other in the queue to point the accusing finger from the witness-stand before it would be pointed at them.

Alfred Hitchcock once said that true terror is when the extraordinary meets the ordinary. That was how the McCarthy terror hit me. It began one morning when I had gone back to our house to collect some of my clothes. The dustbins were overflowing so I set about emptying them. They had to be carried to the bottom of the garden. Old newspapers and magazines were piled separately from the rest of the rubbish. I was just straightening up from dumping a dustbin when I saw two men in raincoats busy sorting through the old news-papers. I was about to ask what they were doing when one of them faced me clutching some crumpled magazines in his hand.

'We'll be keeping these as evidence,' he said, indicating copies of the *Spectator* and *New Statesman*. 'These could be con-sidered subversive literature.'

The second raincoated man stepped forward and pushed a badge under my nose. 'We're from the Federal Bureau of In-vestigation,' he rasped, unfolding a paper from his pocket, 'and we have a warrant to search your house.'

In the face of that shining badge I could not bring myself to utter a word of protest. One hour later, I still had not thought of anything to say as I watched the two men literally take our house apart. Even my weekly laundry lists were not overlooked. Finally, they turned to me again.

'You must hold yourself in readiness to receive a subpoena asking you to attend the court,' said the man with the badge.

I found my voice. 'Do you mind explaining to me what all this is about?'

'Perhaps you didn't know,' he replied, 'but your husband was once a member of the Communist Party of America.'

'That's ridiculous,' I snapped. 'My husband is the least political man I have ever known.'

When I told Loring what had happened at first he could not believe that anyone would ransack his home. Then I told him of the allegation that he had once been a Communist and he began to laugh. Yes, he had been a member of the Communist Party for all of twelve hours and that was over twenty years ago. He was nineteen and still at Harvard. He had got very drunk one night at a students' party and woke up next morning to find a Communist Party membership card in his pocket. He had torn it up not because of any aversion to the Communist ideal, but because the thought of party discipline was abhorrent to him.

Then I told him of their warning that I might be called before the Committee. He made an appointment to see our lawyer, who explained that he doubted whether the two men who had searched our house were FBI agents; more probably they were private detectives posing as such. It was significant that they had called when my husband was out as they must have known how vulnerable I was as an alien, ignorant of my rights. The affair might have been instigated, he guessed, by someone who bore Loring a grudge or even by the FBI itself. But there was no way of proving it one way or the other, so it would be useless for us to complain.

He concluded by saying that Loring's youthful escapade was enough to put him on McCarthy's suspect list. As his wife, it was inevitable that I would be next in the firing line. Cross-examination would reveal the fact of Loring's Mexican divorce and our subsequent marriage in Arizona. Since divorce and marriage laws vary from state to state, our marriage was not valid in California. So far as a Californian court was concerned, Loring and I had been living in sin for the past five years.

'But,' I protested, 'that must apply to thousands of other people.'

'Correct. But thousands of other people are not classified as you are. You are an alien and as such you are liable to the charge of "moral turpitude" to which the American law has one answer, deportation.'

'There's one answer to that,' interjected Loring. 'We'll get married again, right here in Hollywood.'

'I was going to advise that. But don't think that wipes out five years' worth of moral turpitude.'

Loring said that in his opinion we would not even be called upon to testify.

'I'll bet you dollars to doughnuts you're already on their lists,' retorted our lawyer. 'And by the way, what sort of contract have you got with Warner Brothers?'

'It's up for renewal at any time.'

'If those two oafs who called at your house yesterday get around to bending the boss's ear, your contract won't be worth the paper it's written on.'

Two days later Loring came home early from the studios looking like a schoolboy who had just been expelled.

'I can't believe it,' he mumbled. 'The studio chief called me into his office and said my contract is cancelled as of today. No notice. No explanations. Just "You're fired!" '

We were both stunned. For Loring the turn of events was

particularly difficult to grasp. Overnight the 'Bitch-Goddess' had deserted him.

As it turned out, we were only experiencing the effects of the vanguard of the McCarthy terror. His cavalcade had not hit town yet and I was safely back in England before Loring was called upon to testify in the Hollywood trials. But he made up his mind there and then that he was not going to take the easy way out. Despite his youthful brush with the Communist Party, he could still have retrieved his reputation by agreeing to appear as a 'friendly' witness. Instead, he refused to testify against his friends even though such a stand meant jeopardising his future career.

He knew, without a lawyer to tell him, that such an appearance before the Committee meant his name would be blacklisted by all the studios. At only forty, his occupation gone, he faced a bleak future. He was never again to be offered work as a writer in Hollywood. His name was taken off his fine original screenplay for the film *Act of Violence*, which was to win Robert Ryan an Academy Award, and the last news I had of him was that he was courageously building a new career designing swimming pools.

Loring was always more worried about me than about himself. Despite my protests that it was a mockery in the circumstances, he arranged for our immediate marriage or re-marriage. The news about his dismissal from Warner Brothers spread like wildfire. Suddenly our phone stopped ringing. When we tried to find a best man everyone was suddenly too busy or out of town. Mercifully, Tyrone Power came to our rescue. We did not ask him. He volunteered, saying 'I wouldn't dream of seeing a daughter of Cork get married without a fellow Corkian present.' We warned him that his presence might attract the Press. Would he want his name to be associated with a blacklisted writer?

'To hell with 'em all! Big and small!' grinned Power in reply. He saved our second wedding from being the saddest of occasions. It was sad not just because of our broken marriage but because we were both miserably aware that we were already victims of the McCarthy terror and trying to appease a maniac.

But, as always, appeasement did not solve anything. The

next day our lawyer told us that he had heard via the grape-
vine that a warrant commanding my appearance before the
Committee was being prepared and he was sure that the outcome would be my deportation. This would mean a blot on
my passport and almost certainly I would never be permitted
to return to the States. He urged me to do a moonlight flit.

'You still have twenty-four hours. Book a seat on the next
plane out to England or stay and face the consequences. But I
warn you, I shan't be able to help you. That's my last word.'

But it was Loring who had the last word. I questioned him
closely and he admitted that he would eventually marry his
'prospective lady'. The last reason for my remaining in Hollywood had gone.

As it had done when I arrived six years previously, the rain
poured down as I flew out of Hollywood. At New York I
boarded the *Queen Elizabeth* and spent five miserable days
trying to work up some enthusiasm about going home. After
so long an absence, England loomed like a foreign land.

The gloomy dockside of Southampton did nothing to dispel
my sense of alienation. At that time, the customs officials used
to herd incoming passengers into two groups, 'UK Citizens'
and 'Other Nationalities'. To my horror, the little Cockney
porter who was wheeling my luggage was steering a course for
'Other Nationalities'.

'Where do you think you're taking me?' Indignantly I waved
my passport under his nose. 'I'm British!'

With a look of genuine compassion he asked ' 'Ave you been
away long, Miss?'

'Too long!' I blurted out. Tears were pricking my eyelids.

The porter patted me comfortingly on the shoulder. 'Never
mind, Miss,' he said. 'You've come 'ome in time for the National
Sweet Pea Show!'

I could have kissed him. Where else in the world, and from
whom else but a Cockney porter, could I have heard such an
absurdly touching sentence of greeting? As the boat train sped
to London I hugged his words to me. He did not know it, but
he had made me feel at least half-welcomed home.

Chapter 6

Robert

By our first strange and fatal interview
                              John Donne

It seemed natural that when I came home I should think of working with my father. He was now enjoying his greatest success since the Queen Victoria films with Michael Wilding and Anna in *Spring in Park Lane*. Any inhibitions I may have had about not wanting to benefit from his name had now been dispelled by the achievements of my own career. So when he invited me to script his next production, *Trent's Last Case*, I welcomed the chance of getting to know him as a working partner. It was a completely happy experience. With my documentary background and his flair for showmanship, we made a good team. *Trent* starred Margaret Lockwood, Michael Wilding and Orson Welles. It was a very good film but it did my career no good. Although I had added my mother's maiden name to Wilcox in the hope of fending off any charges of nepotism, nobody within the industry would treat me on my own merits. The script had been all my own work, but my father was notorious for lending a hand with his scripts so the reaction was 'Of course the script was good, H. W. wrote it.'

The next film I wrote for him, *King's Rhapsody*, was not a success. So everyone promptly said 'What can you expect if Herbert Wilcox hires his own daughter?' Either way I could not win. H. W. agreed that if I was to further my career we should sever our partnership.

One of the good things that emerged from *Rhapsody* was my meeting with the poet Christopher Hassall, who was also Ivor Novello's lyric writer. I had some capital saved from my Hollywood earnings and decided to set up my own company to produce short films. I would select the subjects, direct and produce, and Hassall would be my writer. It proved a perfect partnership. Our first two films won Edinburgh Awards. The first, *Square Story*, was a fantasy based on the idea of London's statues coming to life, which gave free rein to Hassall's poetic imagination. For the second, *Brighton Story*, I secured Alec Clunes to play the lead and Walter Lassally, who later won fame with *Tom Jones*, to photograph it.

Then I came face to face with a revolutionary change in the policy of film distributors. Cinemascope had just hit the British screens. Three-hour epics became the order of the day, leaving no room in cinema programmes for 'shorts'. I toted my two prize-winning films up and down Wardour Street without finding a distributor willing to book them. The answer was always the same : 'The day of the short film is over.'

After two happy and successful years as an independent film-maker, for the first time in my working life I was unemployed and badly in need of money. Then, quite by chance at a party, I met R. D. Smith, BBC Drama producer and Italia Prize Award winner. To him my unemployment presented no problem. 'Get into TV,' he said. 'The BBC is crying out for talent like yours.'

Six months and many interviews later I had to report to Smith that the 'Beeb' was still not asking for my services. I told him I was sure one of the reasons was that the higher echelons seemed to think that no one was eligible for the 'club' unless he or she had at least one university degree. He hit on a brilliant idea. 'Never mind about filling in any more entry forms that demand an honours degree; take along your own diploma,' he said. 'Make 'em see one of your films.'

I shall always be grateful to Leonard Miall, then head of the TV Talks Department, for agreeing to meet me and view my films. When the lights went up in the projection room, Miall turned to me and said simply, 'Well, how soon can you join us?'

I joined the BBC during its finest years. Under Miall were Donald Baverstock, the originator of *Tonight*, Huw Wheldon, later Managing Director of BBC television, David Attenborough, the naturalist who was to be Head of Programmes for BBC 2, the much loved Norman Swallow, till recently Head of Arts Programmes, Paul Johnstone, the inventor of *Animal, Vegetable, Mineral*, and the witty Nancy Thomas, who was one of only three women (including myself) in the department at the time. Presiding over all was Grace Wyndham Goldie, a woman of powerful intellect combined with a wicked wit.

My immediate working colleagues were also splendid. Stephen Hearst was an Austrian who had fled to England as a refugee from Hitler. He still spoke with an Austrian accent and his favourite phrase when pleased was 'Top Cheers!' He had a slight chip on his shoulder about being a foreigner. One day Stephen and another refugee, Martin Esslin, were overheard in the Bush House canteen commiserating with each other that they, as 'bloody foreigners', would never get far in such a hide-bound organisation as 'Aunty Beeb'. Today, Hearst is Director of Radio Three, while Martin Esslin is Head of Radio Drama and a CBE.

My closest colleague was Richard Cawston, who directed the famous film on the royal family. Grace Wyndham Goldie made the right decision when she teamed me up with Cawston to make documentary films. Of the two of us at the time, I knew more about film-making; but Cawston was to teach me far more than I ever taught him. He approached each production like a military commander planning a campaign and used to plot out the whole film on a large shot-by-shot map on his office wall. It was due to my collaboration with him that within three months of joining the Corporation my name was on the front cover of the *Radio Times*, as one of the directors of a highly successful new documentary series.

After that I branched out on my own with equal success. My work brought me into contact with many writers, including J. B. Priestley, Andrew Sinclair (who made his TV debut under my direction), C. P. Snow and Robert Graves.

I found Graves bewitching. He was terribly nervous of the film medium and told me bluntly on the first morning of shooting that if he did not like it he would walk out. His preconceived idea of film-making was that it was 'a most unpeaceful activity'. However, he sailed through take after take without a fluff. But at the end of the first day he left the set abruptly giving no indication whether he would be back the next day or not. Going into my office the next morning before daring to go on the set, I found a book on my desk. It was the latest anthology of Robert Graves. In the fly-leaf he had written: 'With gratitude and admiration for giving me a most peaceful experience. Robert Graves.'

C. P. Snow was to present a different kind of problem when I was assigned to direct him in a film called *Return to Cambridge*, which was to look back at his life and career. I discovered C. P. to be basically a shy man and on the morning he arrived in Cambridge for the first day's shooting, I think he would have got on the next train back to London had it not been for the comforting presence of his wife, Pamela Hansford Johnson. He did not at first take easily to direction and the inevitable exercise of repeating the same action over and over again irritated him. The tension was such that the crew irreverently nicknamed him 'The Abominable Snowman'. This was unfair. He was not purposely being difficult. It was simply a case of not knowing the tiresome mechanics of film-making. However, behind his somewhat awesome exterior C. P. has great personal charm and by the second day this broke through, and he was asking the sound man to explain his problems and exchanging opinions with the cameraman. The crew was completely won over, and so I believe was C. P. At any rate, he gave a first-class performance and said he was delighted with the finished film.

It was part of the ritual in Leonard Miall's department that he read annual progress reports to each member of his staff. What made me as happy as any success I had at the 'Corp' was the fact that for three consecutive years my report always ended with the words 'Pamela Wilcox is very well liked by all her colleagues.' Then, when everything seemed set fair for a long and successful career, it happened.

At a very early age I discovered Robert Frost's poem 'The Path Not Taken'. It sums up my philosophy as a fatalist. On looking back it always seems that the really important things that have happened to me have occurred by accident rather than design. And so it was with my reunion with Robert.

On New Year's Eve I got home early from the BBC to prepare for an evening which offered at least three parties. But I felt an odd hesitation about getting changed, combined with an inner exultation which New Year's Eve always invokes in me. I had moved into a lovely studio flat in Tite Street which had once belonged to Augustus John. From the bedroom windows I could see the twinkling lights of Battersea Pleasure Gardens. On an impulse, I pulled on my coat and a few minutes later found myself climbing the familiar Tree Walk which was suspended among the trees high above the noise and music of the fair. I stood for a moment listening to the chimes of Chelsea church, joined by the faint echo of Big Ben which drifted down the river. As I listened I remembered some lines from an Auden poem which, long ago, Robert had read to me :

> But all the clocks in the City
> Began to whirr and chime :
> O let not Time deceive you,
> You cannot conquer Time . . .

I wondered what had become of Robert in the ten years since we had last met at Denham. I knew that he had become a famous film director and had heard that he and Jane had parted.

The hurdy-gurdy music from the roundabouts below struck up a premature version of 'Auld Lang Syne', and suddenly I saw him walking towards me with his familiar long, ambling gait. We stood staring at each other in amazement for a few seconds. Then he reached out and grasped both my hands in his. 'Welcome home !' he said.

Although I had been back from America for more than four years, it seemed that ever since my return I had been waiting for someone to say just that to me.

'It's been a long time between drinks,' he said, still holding my hands. 'Do you still guzzle Coca-Cola ?'

I nodded.

'Well,' he said, 'as it's New Year's Eve, do you think you

might jump on my wagon long enough to let me buy you a glass of champers?'

Typically, Robert took charge of our destination. We went to the bar of the Caprice restaurant. And we talked. How we talked! The years of separation were filled in and swept away as if we had parted only the previous day. At eleven o'clock I vaguely mentioned a party. 'To hell with parties!' retorted Robert. 'I can't think of anyone with whom I would rather spend New Year's Eve!'

At half past eleven he hustled me into a taxi. 'I've told the driver to take us to a favourite haunt of mine,' he said. 'And after tonight I have more fondness than ever for it . . . the Garden of Eden I call it from now on.'

We went back to Battersea Pleasure Gardens. Standing on the floodlit Tree Walk, we looked out over the Thames and as Big Ben struck midnight we wished each other a happy new year. Then he took both my hands in his.

'When I'm free,' he said, 'you're going to marry me.'

'You've had too much champers,' I said, without believing it.

'My dearest girl,' he replied, 'one of the things you don't know about me is my infinite capacity for consuming alcohol. I've a theory I was born several hundred drinks under par, so I'm always catching up.'

At that moment I could not be expected to realise the sadly prophetic nature of his words. All I knew was that within those few hours my feelings for Robert as the idolised friend of my adolescence had changed into the complete love of an adult.

Life with Robert was like sharing life with three or four different men. Even his appearance was ambivalent. He had the long aquiline face of a poet, and, although not tall, the perfectly proportioned body of a light-weight boxer. Coming from a middle-class family in Yorkshire, he had won a scholarship to Cambridge where he gained a double first in history and mathematics. His flair for mathematics had shown itself at an early age. As a boy of seven he had gone in great excitement to his father believing that he had invented a new mathematical formula. When his father broke the news to him that somebody had already invented the decimal system, he burst into tears. But his overriding passion was poetry. He let me read some of the poems he had written at Cambridge. If films had not caught his imagination, he might well, I believe, have become a major poet.

One of the most compelling traits of his personality was his amazing zest for life. Often a single day's programme would include listening to and reading the score of a Mozart opera, an afternoon's matinée of *Hamlet* at the Old Vic, a dip into a Marx Brothers' film in the evening and on to a jazz club until dawn. All these activities were washed down with an inordinate amount of what he fondly called 'alc'. His 'alc' timetable would begin before breakfast with a couple of lagers. By eleven he would be opening the wine which he drank like water until lunch-time, when he would move on to haunts like the Screen Writers Club and the hard stuff. Then it was on to the Garrick followed by a string of after-lunch brandies which would last until five o'clock when it was time for the evening whisky session, which often went on until dawn.

Yet never once during the beginning of our relationship did I see him show signs of being drunk. It seemed to me that there must be something in his theory about being born several drinks under par. I should have realised that even his cast-iron constitution could not stand the strain indefinitely. This was the core of Robert's tragedy. Alcohol had bitten so deeply into his mental and physical being that when it finally caught up with him it was too late.

During our early days together there was not even a shadow of the tragedy that was to overtake us. Ironically, my only misgivings lay in the fact that I believed he would have been happier if I could have been more of a drinking partner. But the price I always had to pay was the most horrible hangover. This should have been a warning to me, but I disregarded it. If, as the doctors said, Robert was the classic case of an incurable alcoholic, then I was the classic case of the opposite because I could only take so much without becoming ill.

The difference between our twin downfalls was that I could have avoided mine. Robert could not. Yet, totally unlike a typical drunk, who gets mean and violent in his cups, Robert was always the gentlest and most compassionate of men. Documentary film producer Harry Watt said after his death 'Robert was the best loved man in the film industry. Even at the time of his decline, when he appeared drunk on the set, the lowest electrician did his best to shield him.'

Robert had moved into my flat in Tite Street, and we planned to marry as soon as possible. Jane was now living abroad but Robert told her of our relationship. He sensed she was still emotionally dependent on him and had not yet raised the subject of divorce. He was planning to fly out to her to solve the problem when we were faced with unforeseeable tragedy. Jane fell and injured her spine. Two weeks later Robert returned from visiting her in Roehampton Hospital. 'How could I tell her that she will never walk again,' he asked me, 'and in the next breath ask her for a divorce?'

It was an insoluble situation. I felt our relationship was sufficiently strong not to need legal support. But Robert brooded on the possibility that we could never be married. Basically a sentimentalist, he saw marriage as a symbolic way of proclaiming love.

He solved this problem with a typically romantic plan, which was sparked off by the arrival in England of the great Italian film director Vittorio De Sica. They admired each other enormously and, although De Sica could speak little English, they delighted in each other's company. This delight reached its apex in their joint admiration for the work of Hogarth. To celebrate De Sica's birthday, Robert proposed that we should take him to Chiswick churchyard where Hogarth lay buried.

In the morning, before we picked up De Sica, Robert went down on one knee in front of me. Fumbling in his pocket, he produced a beautiful ring set with opals (which are my birthstone) and diamonds.

'Will you marry me today at Hogarth's church?' he asked. Then he told me his plan. Chiswick church was very close to his heart, not only on account of Hogarth, but because it was one of London's most beautiful small churches. It would be empty at noon and Robert's plan was that we should sneak inside and, with De Sica standing in as padre, we would be married, as he put it, 'in the sight of God and Hogarth'.

The plan appealed to my romantic feelings, but I was dubious about its operation and said as much to Robert and

De Sica. 'Supposing the real padre put in an appearance?' I objected.

'Bugger the padre,' said Robert.

'Buggah il padre,' chimed in De Sica, grinning with the happiness of a child who had been invited to join a party game.

It was a perfect spring morning when we climbed out of the taxi at the entrance to Chiswick church. Daffodils crowded Hogarth's simple tomb with the epitaph by David Garrick.

De Sica swept off his black beret and turned to Robert.

'Please,' he said, 'read it for me . . . what a great actor has said about the greatest of painters.'

Slowly, Robert began to read what must be one of the most moving epitaphs ever written :

> 'Farewell, great Painter of Mankind
> Who reached the noblest point of Art.
> Whose pictured morals charm the mind
> And through the eye, correct the heart.
> If Genius fire thee, Reader stay !
> If Nature touch thee, drop a tear.
> If neither moves thee, turn away
> For Hogarth's honoured dust lies here !'

'The line I like most,' said Robert, 'is "And through the eye, correct the heart".'

'For me,' said De Sica, his eyes brimming with tears, 'I like, "If Nature touch thee, drop a tear".'

With one hand he brushed the tears from his cheek, and with his still wet forefinger he bent forward and drew a tiny sign of the cross on the tombstone. Then Robert took my hand and we walked to the entrance of the glowing little church. But, alas, we were not to enter. We found both doors firmly locked.

Without a word De Sica took us by the hand and led us back to Hogarth's tomb. 'What better altar could you wish?' he asked simply. Then he reached into his pocket for the ring. 'Do you, Roberto, take this woman, Pamilia . . . Do you, Pamilia, take this man Roberto until death do you part?'

And so we were 'married'.

Chapter 7

The Slide

*Every alcoholic, consciously or unconsciously, has a
'rendezvous with death'.*
                              Scott Fitzgerald

Human memory is kind. It draws a curtain over the exact
chronology of misery. My memory of Robert's slide into alcoholism is a series of signposts. I remember, for instance, the
first time his speech began to slur, the first time his legs gave
way and he had to be carried to a taxi, the first of the morning
trembling fits which were so violent he could hardly lift the
customary glass of lager to his lips. These signals acted on
Robert not as a warning, but as a challenge. He panicked into
thinking that more liquor would overcome these unexplainable
weaknesses.

Then came the day when he collapsed on the film set. This
was the first time even a hint of his illness had encroached on
his professional life. But the reaction of the studio chiefs was
unanimous. They demanded his resignation from the film.
They would most certainly have won if it had not been for
the affection and loyalty of Terry Thomas, who announced
that if Robert left he would walk out too.

Sadly, the film did not fulfil Thomas's faith. The general
verdict in the trade press was that it was very much below
the standard expected from such a brilliant director. The film
industry is a cruel gossip-shop and the men who run it have
short memories. For the first time in his career Robert found
himself without offers for future work. This situation produced
in him a most uncharacteristic state of depression which led to

even heavier drinking. The outcome was predictable, but none the less terrifying when it actually happened.

I was at home in Tite Street working on a BBC script which I was to begin filming the next day. I was not expecting Robert home until later. Our daily routine had fallen into a pattern of Robert going off in the evenings to his drinking haunts and, I would hope, coming home sober enough to eat the meal which I had prepared for him. It was about seven o'clock when I heard his key in the door. He walked towards me steadily enough, but his face was deadly white and his eyes looked glazed.

'Go out and see if I've fastened the lift door properly and check if the lift is still there.'

It was not like him to issue peremptory orders but the urgency of his voice made me obey him. When I came back he was sitting huddled in a chair, his face buried in his hands. Without looking up he asked 'Has the lift gone?'

'Yes.'

He shuddered. 'Thank God!'

I knelt by his side. 'Robert, what is the matter?'

'For God's sake, pour me a drink. Then I'll tell you.'

After a long swig at his drink, the colour began to come back into his face.

'Now tell me,' I said.

He gave a short, mirthless laugh. 'Either I'm going off my head, or . . .' He buried his face in his hands again, unable to finish the sentence. Then, with an obvious effort to pull himself together, he began to tell me what had happened. He spoke in sharp, staccato sentences, like a child recounting a nightmare.

Before going to the Screen Writers Club he had decided, as it was a lovely evening, to take a walk. As usual he had gone to our favourite haunt, Battersea Gardens. He was sitting on a seat by the lake when he first saw it. At first he thought it was a waterlogged kite washed up on the water's edge. Then, as he watched, it emerged dripping on the pavement. It was a giant lobster. It sat still for a few minutes waving its claws, then started to crawl straight towards him.

'The thing that horrified me most,' he said, 'was not that it was making for me, but that it was lame.' He shuddered. 'It dragged one giant claw behind it, making a grating noise along the pavement. Somehow the fact that it was lame made it seem more obscene. It went on crawling towards me until it was close enough to my feet for me to have reached down and touched it. Then it stopped in its tracks, staring up at me and waving its huge front claws, like a praying mantis.'

Robert took a long, shuddering pull at his drink, then he went on. 'It stopped praying and clawed at my shoe. It started to climb up my trouser leg. I struck out at it. Then I must have blacked out. When I came to I was still sitting on the seat. It had gone, but I could still see the wet trail leading up to my shoe.'

He broke off and silently I went to put my arm around him, but he brushed me aside.

'Wait,' he cried, 'that's not the worst of it. I had started to walk back here when I heard it following me. There was no mistaking the dragging sound of that lame claw. I said to myself "I won't look back." And I didn't, not until I reached the main road. "It will never get through the traffic," I said to myself. And so then I looked back. God damn its eyes, it was crawling across the pedestrian crossing with all the bloody traffic waiting for it.'

Perspiration was standing out in beads on Robert's forehead. I tried to stop him. I did not want to hear any more. But doggedly he went on.

'It followed me round the corner, right to the front-door and into the lift. When we reached this floor it was still there. As I left the lift I heard its dragging claw close behind me. That's when I shut the gates on it. God, I heard it scream!'

He was now pacing the floor of the flat and stopped only to pour himself another drink.

'Darling,' I said quietly, 'you must see a doctor at once.'

'God damn it, I don't need a quack to tell me what's wrong with me! I've had the DTs.' He swallowed some of his drink. 'Let's hope "had" is the right tense. God, I can't believe it's happened to me!'

That night he did not sleep at all. I could feel him beside me, wide awake, waiting for the terror to come again. At seven o'clock he was up.

'I'm going for a walk,' he said, 'and let's hope it's a solitary one.'

'I'm coming with you,' I said. 'And when we get home we'll get hold of a good doctor.'

'Only if I see it again,' he said.

He led me straight to Battersea Gardens and we sat down on the same seat.

'Any sign of it?' I asked.

He shook his head and got to his feet abruptly. We began walking home and were just leaving the gardens when suddenly he stiffened and stopped in his tracks.

'There it is again,' he said. 'Can't you hear it?' He appealed to me like a child. I shook my head.

'Listen, it's still dragging its claw,' he said, trembling violently.

'Look over your shoulder,' I said. 'There's nothing there.'

Obediently he looked back and then turned to me with a half-smile, half-sob.

'All right, you win. It's the doc for me. The damned thing's been out and pupped. There are two of them now.'

I shall always be grateful to Donald Taylor, the producer of *Sparrows Can't Sing*, for introducing us to Dr Kemp, who did more than any one person to prolong Robert's life, although he was too late to save it. Kemp was a leading specialist in the cure of alcoholics. Robert offered little initial resistance and Kemp at once arranged for a drying-out process in a nursing home.

'Robert's not to blame for his alcoholism,' Kemp said, 'any more than you would blame a man born with one leg shorter than the other for limping. The tragedy is that it has taken so long for him to collapse. I cannot guarantee any cure.'

The first morning I went to visit Robert at the nursing home Kemp refused to let me see him.

'He wouldn't want you or anyone to see him in this state,' said Kemp. 'I've had to put him into a strait-jacket.'

'Is it the lame lobster?' I asked.

'Hundreds of them,' replied Kemp. 'And he thinks they're attacking his genitals.'

The first drying-out period lasted four weeks. Robert came out much shaken and for three weeks did not drink at all. But

F

total abstinence was obviously torture for him and despite the
help of Kemp's drugs he was soon drinking just as heavily
again. After that, the drying-out periods, alternating with
periods of heavy drinking, became a regular pattern. Shortly
after this Dr Kemp died of cancer and Robert lost a great
friend and his one hope of recovery. Kemp had taught him to
realise that he was mortally ill. He knew it with every drink
he took, with every drying-out cure. But he faced it with great
courage and never ceased to fight back.

I remember once, after many attempts at drying-out, I asked
him if this or any bout was as bad as the first encounter with
the lame lobster. He was looking strangely young in a hospital
gown, which had only just replaced a strait-jacket.

'No,' he said, with his whimsical, sad laugh. 'But "After the
first death there is no other." '

It is difficult to date the time when I first started drinking
seriously. It was a gradual process prompted by the increasing
misery of Robert's condition. When he was drinking it now
seemed less painful to drink with him than to watch in cold
sobriety while he poisoned himself. When he was drying out,
I continued drinking to help me forget about his agony. My
intake never equalled his, but I was drinking enough to make
me feel ill most of the time. I was always on edge, and so my
relationship with my BBC colleagues deteriorated and the
quality of my work suffered.

The first to notice was Leonard Miall. He sent for me one
morning and, without the subject of drink being mentioned,
he suggested that I needed a holiday. Why didn't I take two
months off on full pay? Instead of accepting I reacted with
angry defiance. I did not need a rest. There was nothing wrong
with my work that a good script would not cure. I am sure he
was not deceived or reassured by my protests, but I had put
him in an intolerable position and, being the gentle man he is,
he only replied sadly 'Well, don't say I haven't warned
you.'

Meanwhile, my private life was moving from crisis to crisis.
Robert had been declared bankrupt on almost the same date as

my father. H. W.'s bankruptcy was not brought about by personal failure, but was endemic to the flagging fortunes of the British film industry. Bankruptcy hit my father hard but he refused to admit defeat and continued working harder than ever to rebuild his career. As a result, he suffered a coronary and nearly died. Although I had never been dependent on H. W. financially, he represented the one solid bastion of my life and his collapse was a terrible blow. In addition, many of my closest friends died at this time, Christopher Hassall, Alec Clunes, Alan Rawsthorne, Donald Taylor – all were relatively young but in the space of a year they were all dead. Finally, within weeks of each other, my step-father and my mother had died, both of cancer. It seemed like an avalanche of death which I was to feel all the more keenly in the near future when I would need friends as I had never needed them before.

I made two films in a row which the BBC rated as flops. My successful career in the film department was finished. My last interview with Leonard Miall was even more painful for him than it was for me. Once again the true cause of my failure was not mentioned. Leonard suggested that the time had come when, for both our sakes, a parting of the ways would be best. The frustrations of Corporation life were cramping my talents. But for all his tact, the message was simple and blunt : I was fired. As I left his room I said to myself 'After six of the happiest years of my professional life, I am closing the door on my career. Can this really be happening to me?'

The next few months are a blur of unreality. I tried to avoid facing the facts and lived from one hangover to the next. With Dr Kemp's death, Robert had temporarily given up taking any cures and together we fell into a period of alcoholic self-pity, clinging to one another in mutual misery. Eventually, our money began to run out. I felt much too low to apply for a job in TV or films, even if work had been available. Untrained in anything but films, I eventually took the first job I thought practical, which was selling advertising space over the telephone. No wonder Fleet Street calls its telephone sales staff their scullery-maids. It was a demanding, demeaning job paying only a paltry salary, and I hated it. Soon the newspaper folded and I was out of a job again. At that time Robert was trying a new cure of treatment by drugs. He was prescribed a medicine which was supposed to make him sick at even the smell of a drink. The cure was self-administered and my chief memory of those weeks of unemployment, living in the one shabby room to which we had now moved, is of Robert continually being sick. Eventually he gave up and the cupboard above our wash-basin was full of the bottles of dark brown medicine. It was that collection of bottles that was to end our life together.

One Friday I had just got home after wearily doing the rounds of employment agencies and was preparing a meal, when there was a knock at the door. 'Oh, God!' I thought, 'it's the landlady again, after the rent which we haven't got.' But it was Robert. He had forgotten his key. He was steady on his feet, but I noticed a strange smell on his breath. I thought it was rum, but rum was the one drink he never touched. 'What have you been drinking?' I demanded.

He produced a bottle of the dark brown medicine from his overcoat pocket. 'My medicine!' he said, and with a flourish he pulled out the cork and drained the bottle in one gulp and went to throw it into the waste-paper basket. I grabbed it from him and sniffed it. There was no longer any doubt. The bottle had been filled with rum.

'What in God's name do you think you're doing?' I cried.

Robert stood looking at me like a shamefaced schoolboy, then he said lamely 'Trying to deceive you. Rum's the same colour.'

I crossed to the wash-basin cupboard and opened it. 'Are all these full of rum too?'

'I'm afraid so,' he said dejectedly.

Never before in all our seven years together had he tried to deceive me. That it was such a pathetic deception did not make his action seem any more forgivable. Not trusting myself to speak, I took the bottles from the cabinet and one by one emptied the contents down the lavatory.

'Be careful you don't throw the baby out with the bath-water!' He snatched the last bottle from my hand, pulled out the cork and sniffed. 'This one's the real thing.' He grinned sheepishly, and with a shudder took a swig.

'Take it then,' I said, 'and get out of here!'

He looked at me as if I'd slapped his face, then he said plead-
ingly 'I can't get out right now.' He pointed to the medicine
bottle. 'I'll have to stay and be sick first.'

'Go and be sick in the gutter,' I said. 'Go and be sick anywhere in the world. But not here !'

He paled. 'Are you giving me my marching orders ?'

My anger had gone. I wanted to put my arm round him,
but instead I nodded.

'I can't blame you,' he said in a low voice. 'You can't be
half as sick of me as I am of myself.' With a grimace he put
the medicine bottle in his pocket and slowly began to walk towards the door. The urge to put my arms round his dejected
shoulders was hard to resist. But I made no move towards him.
The next moment the door closed softly behind him. I was
alone.

For four days I did not dare move out of the room in case he
came back or the telephone rang. On the fifth day my pride,
which had prevented me from calling any of his friends, gave
way to fear for his safety. A dozen calls all proved blank. Finally
I tracked down one of his close friends, who had bad news.
Robert had come to him and borrowed fifty pounds, saying
that I had turned him out and he was penniless. Against his
better judgement, the friend had given him the money. Two days
later he had received a call from Robin Maugham. Robert had
turned up at his flat in Brighton in a hired car with a chauffeur.
He was very drunk and confessed that he had not eaten for
days. He had refused Maugham's invitation to stay the night,
and when Maugham went to see him off to some unknown
destination, he had noticed that the back of the car had been
filled with empty whisky bottles.

What happened to him during the following weeks no one
can tell for certain. The last person to see him alive was an
old Cambridge friend. Robert had arrived in his hired car with
the now bewildered chauffeur. His friend had invited him in
because he thought Robert was ill. He tried in vain to urge
him to go to the local hospital. Then he took the chauffeur
aside, and, after paying the bill for a week's hire of the car,

persuaded him to deliver Robert to a hospital as soon as they reached London.

It was exactly six weeks after he left our room that I received a telegram : HOW COULD YOU LEAVE ME WITHOUT MY CLOAK. I LOVE YOU. ROBERT. The telegram was stamped London, but there was no address or telephone number to which I could reply.

That same afternoon my landlady threatened immediate eviction unless I paid the rent. To escape her I went for a walk along the Kings Road and stopped at the newsagent's to pick up my copy of the *Telegraph*. It was three o'clock in the afternoon when I entered Lyons and ordered a sandwich and a cup of coffee. I had just realised I was hungry. I had not eaten properly for days. I opened the *Telegraph* to study the 'Sits Vac' pages, and saw Robert's face smiling up at me from the obituary page. Then the headline jumped out at me : 'Famous Film Director dies.'

When George Gershwin died at forty, his friend John O'Hara is reported to have said 'I read in the papers that Gershwin is dead. But I don't have to believe it if I don't want to.'

That's how it was with me. I sat there reading and re-reading the glowing tribute, which ended with the bare statement that he had died in hospital.

I suddenly noticed it was growing dark. My sandwich and coffee were untouched. Then I thought 'What I need is a drink,' and with the paper under my arm I found myself sitting at a bar. I downed one brandy, then another, and another. On my empty stomach I should have felt some effect. But I remained sober. The next thing I remember is walking up the street back to my room. My key turned in the lock but the door would not budge. Perhaps I was tight after all. Then I noticed an envelope pinned to the door. It was a note from my landlady telling me that my luggage had been removed from my room, which was double-locked and would remain so. Pending payment of my rent, she was retaining my belongings.

As I stood facing the locked door for a few moments, even my grief was engulfed by a survival instinct. What was my next move? Where and to whom could I turn? Coldly, rationally, the possibilities raced through my mind.

My father? No, that was out of the question. He was still gravely ill. My brother or sisters? Thanks to my seven years in America, during a formative time in our lives, we were virtually strangers. I had not seen John since he was called up early in the war to serve with the army photographic unit. Paddy was in the final stages of an unhappy marriage and Sheila was in Australia. No, there was no solution on the family side. What about friends? How many of us can honestly say that they know more than two or three individuals who they could turn to with the wreckage that my life now was? My last bastion, Grierson, was away in India. Most of those who had known both Robert and me were now dead. What about former BBC colleagues? There is, perhaps, no severance quite so final as dismissal under disgrace from 'Auntie Beeb'. Only three people kept in touch: the writer Allan Prior, the journalist Romany Bain, and Nancy Thomas, a producer. They had shown me great kindness and because of this I did not feel I could call on them yet again.

As for my financial resources, all I had was the few pounds in my bag.

I felt like a chess player who can trace his defeat right back to the first move of the game. Everyone has his breaking point. I had reached mine.

As I turned away from that locked door, it crossed my mind to try asking my landlady to release my luggage. But what use was luggage when I did not even know where I was going? I still had no idea when I found myself walking through the growing darkness. Nor did I know how long I had been walking when I stopped at a cross-roads. Panic seized me. I was lost. But could one get lost in London in so short a space of time? Or was it so short? It had been twilight when I left my lodgings. Now it was dark, and I was in an unfamiliar street with no landmark in sight. Suddenly I thought I must invent a destination for myself. I was on my way to Victoria. Yes, that was it. There was no reason for my choice. It was the first landmark that came into my head.

I do not know how long I had been walking round in circles when I found myself sitting in Parliament Square facing the policeman's torch.

'But all the clocks in the City began to whirr and chime. . . .' In the darkness outside the windowless attic of the hostel in which I now lay, a clock was striking four. As I tried to turn over in the narrow bed, the metal disc that Bloody Mary had placed around my neck pressed against my skin.

In the next bed a woman was crying in her sleep. Why could I not cry, I wondered. I was now Number Twenty-two and Robert was dead. Perhaps I was too tired for tears. I pulled the grey blankets up to my chin. The overpowering smell of carbolic flooded my nostrils like chloroform. What was it the anaesthetist had told me as a frightened child? 'Count from ten backwards.' My eyelids were already closing as I started to count in a whisper. 'Ten, nine, eight, seven.' Then, mercifully, came oblivion.

Chapter 8

The Padlock and Chain

The exact nature of despair is simply this. It does not know it is despair.
            Soren Kierkegaard

A minute or so later, or so it seemed, I was aware of a violent pain inside my head. A fire-bell was ringing. So far as I was concerned, the place could burn down. I had to sleep. Pulling the blankets over my head, I sank back. A second later the blankets were ripped from my body and a hand descended on my bare buttocks with the force of a horse dealer. 'Wakey! Wakey!' I opened my eyes to see Bloody Mary bending over me. 'Wakey! Wakey!' she shrieked again, whirling her keys over my prostrate body. Then she passed on down the dormitory, calling out at the top of her voice 'Wakey, wakey, girls! Rise and shine!'

Within the next few minutes bedlam broke loose. The grey shrouded shapes rose, stumbling out of their beds, and scrambled into their clothes. Cursing, swearing, still only half dressed, they began a stampede for the door.

Using my raincoat as a dressing gown, I was struggling to dress so that I could get out and above all escape from the bell. Suddenly, it stopped.

In the relative quiet that followed, I realised that the woman kneeling by the next bed was praying aloud. Garbed from head to foot in black, she made the sign of the cross, pulled the black veil forward over her white hair, then, still kneeling, she began silently and reverently to gather together a Bible, a posy of pressed, faded Parma violets, a signet ring, and finally a faded photograph of a man dressed in First World War uniform. All these objects she tenderly stowed away in a plastic bag along with face cloth, toothbrush and soap. Then, after adjusting the long black veil so as to obscure her face completely, she rose and, clutching her plastic bag, the Black Widow, as she was called, glided silently out of my life. Or so I thought.

The occupant of the bed on my right was known as Peg-Leg, which, as I soon learned from her, was a title that came in handy in the world of homeless women, where so many seemed to have nicknames. Perhaps they were a protection against anonymity, because the rules of some hostels dictated that one was addressed by number and not by name.

I was about to slip into my skirt when a rattle of keys signalled the approach of Bloody Mary.

'Whoever threw them blankets on the floor, pick 'em up!'

I pretended not to hear. My skirt was ripped out of my hands.

'I said pick up them blankets!'

'Do what the old cow says.'

The raucous whisper came from Peg-Leg, who was fastening irons on her crippled leg. I recognised the voice of experience and obeyed. As I was bending over the pile of stinking blankets, Bloody Mary's keys flicked like a cat-o'-nine-tails across the back of my bare thighs.

'How dare you!' I cried.

'Cool down now!' muttered Peg-Leg.

Bloody Mary turned on me savagely. 'Just who do you think you are?'

'A human being,' I replied.

Bloody Mary hooted with laughter.

'That's a good one, that is! A human being! Well, let me tell you something, Twenty-two. Here, we go by numbers. You obey orders or you get out.'

'I'm getting out,' I said, ripping the yellow disc from my neck. 'Just as soon as I've had a bath.'

'A bath!' sneered Bloody Mary. 'You'll be lucky!' She shoved my disc into her pocket.

Peg-Leg saved the situation. She gave me a friendly wink and took my arm.

'All right, Mary. Once through the washhouse will take the starch out of this one.'

'Yes, but first she does the toilets,' said Bloody Mary.

'But Twenty-three's on toilets today,' said Peg-Leg.

'Number Twenty-two does the toilets today.'

Peg-Leg started to propel me to the door.

'Come on or we'll miss our turn at the taps.'

The descent to the washhouse seemed as endless as the previous night's ascent to the dormitory. Peg-Leg led the way, tapping her iron boot against the stone stairs with vigorous agility.

We reached the basement and Peg-Leg's cackle was lost in the roar of an all-female underwater inferno. No flames, no sulphur; just dirty water everywhere, dripping from the ceiling, streaming down the sides of the concrete walls, flowing in rivulets of dirty soap-suds underfoot, and punctuated by the monotonous sound of flushing lavatories.

It was a macabre spectacle. Over 100 women going through their daily ablutions, in conditions to which no self-respecting farmer would expose his pigs. There were two lavatories and one rusty bath-tub. In contrast, there was no shortage of carbolic soap, which, I later learned, is used for washing, shampooing, laundering and stair-cleaning.

Allowing for the older or slower-footed and subtracting five minutes for descending and ascending eight flights of stairs, the morning washing period for 150 women lasts about ten minutes and is the reason for the stampede which begins at 5.30 a.m. at the first note of the fire-bell. The washhouse can be the battlefield of the hostel world. The two objectives are the tap line and the clothes-line.

The tap line at the Padlock and Chain consists of ten hot and ten cold taps on either side of the concrete walls. No hand-basins. The water, dirty or clean, runs directly into gulleys cut out of the stone floor. That morning there were three women to each tap and, out of a queue of thirty, about three managed to reach the rusty bath-tub.

The battle of the clothes-line generally takes place at the

same time. The network of clothes-lines made from string or rope is strung up haphazardly, like a cat's cradle. There is a pecking order governing the best corners for airing. Trespassing or 'borrowing' space is not permitted. That morning a woman weighing over twenty stone was garrotting her victim with the jealously guarded clothes-line on which the unsuspecting newcomer had hung her underwear. Only Peg-Leg's iron boot saved her.

Upstairs the bright sunlight of early spring was filtering through the barred peep-hole of the formidable front door, making the dingy hallway seem less forbidding than on the previous night. Bloody Mary was not seated behind her wooden cubby-hole but the sight of that heavy metal key-ring hanging on its hook was a reminder of her presence. Yet even that did not look quite so sinister, hanging against the green, peeling paint. The daylight had revealed the hidden element of colour, a green which for me will forever spell out the word 'hostel'. It is splashed over most pages of Mayhew's *London Labour and the Poor*, when, in Victorian England, it covered alms-houses, jails, doss-houses, work-houses, almost the total architectural map of the poor stretching from Shepherd Market to Bermondsey Docks. Perhaps the origin of the choice was philanthropic, invoking a touch of nature's paintbrush to brighten the existence of those who lived out their brief lives without ever seeing a blade of grass, let alone a tree. At the Padlock and Chain it succeeded in making the entrance less like a prison and more like a seedy boarding-house.

But why had I not taken Bert's advice sooner? 'Kip and skip'? I could have escaped two hours ago. The notion of escape made my heart thump with apprehension. Even before I got to the door, I knew it would be bolted; and even before I had wrestled with the bolts, I knew it would also be locked.

'Where do you think you're going?'

I turned to see Bloody Mary emerging from a door on one side of the narrow entrance hall.

Trying to keep my voice steady, I said :

'Will you please unlock the front door? I'm leaving.'

'You'll leave when everyone else leaves, at 8.30. Not a minute before, not a minute later.'

'I'll wait here,' I said.

'You'll wait in the waiting-room, like everyone else! Or I'll fetch the Super to you!'

'Fetch the Super,' I retorted childishly. 'I'm staying here.'

For a moment the pebble-hard eyes faltered. Then, she leaned over the rail of the staircase.

'Elsie! I want the stairs done early starting here, at the bottom. Bring an extra mop and I'll give you a hand.'

A mouse-like girl came clumping up the stairs carting a mop and bucket.

'I said two mops!' snapped Bloody Mary.

The girl muttered something. Bloody Mary paid no heed, but seized the sopping mop and in one sweeping movement swooshed a rivulet of soapy water over my ankles.

'Go on,' she directed the bewildered girl, thrusting the mop into her hand. 'What are you waiting for?'

The girl looked as though she was going to burst into tears. Bloody Mary snatched the mop and started a mopping movement around my feet, then, with her free hand, she pushed open the dark green door.

'No keys!' she said, as she pushed me inside. 'In you go!'

My first impression of the waiting-room was that I had intruded on a seance. Women were seated, singly or in little groups, around the room, immobile as figures in a waxworks. Every head was turned in the direction of a large clock on the wall at the far end of the room. It was just striking eight.

My second impression, as the door slammed behind me, was of silence. This silence, punctuated only by the ticking of the wall clock, was more frightening than the rattle of Bloody Mary's keys or the frenzy of the washhouse because it was so unexpected, so alien to a gathering of women anywhere.

The silent group was composed of the same individuals who less than half an hour ago had been squabbling over their clothes-line rights or queueing up stark naked for their turn at the tap line. They looked so ordinary, so respectable, like a typical women's outing waiting for the arrival of a charabanc to take them to the seaside. But although they were preparing for a journey, their luggage was not right. Some had shopping bags crammed full of possessions, with perhaps a pair of unwearable shoes or a cheap plastic sponge bag half-hidden under some knitting. Others had on their knees or tucked under their chairs paper carriers, or small neatly-wrapped parcels clutched in their hands or stuffed into coat pockets.

Yet there were all the signs of women preparing for a special occasion as they concentrated on their anxious last-minute titivations.

I took a closer look at the woman seated nearest the window. For the third time she took out a little mirror from her worn, bulging handbag, adjusted the angle of a sad little hat, ascertained that the scottie brooch in her lapel was securely fastened. Then, as for the third time she dusted her shiny nose with a grubby shred of powder-puff, I caught a glimpse of the expression in her eyes reflected in the pocket-mirror. It was an expression that had nothing to do with vanity, an expression that one shudders to see in the eyes of a woman of any age anywhere in the world. Fear. Stark, haunting fear.

Furtively, she put the mirror away in her handbag, as if she was also trying to put away her fear. I followed the nervous gesture of her worn hands as she put on her left glove. As she did so, the other glove dropped to the floor. I bent down to pick it up and it was only then that I realised it was another left-hand glove and the colour did not quite match. So as not to embarrass her I looked at the floor, and quickly she drew back her right foot, revealing that the carefully polished shoe had a large hole in the sole padded with newspaper.

The waiting-room was full of women like this who were trying to hide – from each other, from themselves, from the world – the badges of their despair.

Then suddenly the whole room moved into focus and I noticed something else. Almost all the women were sitting with their backs to the light. In contrast to the windowless tomb of their nights, the predominant feature of the waiting-room was a long curtainless window. No one looked out of the window. Everyone seemed to pretend it did not exist.

But people passing by looked in from the pavement outside. Some with derision, a few with pity. So when the milkman called out to the woman with the scottie brooch ' 'Allo Mum, see we've got our best 'at on today!' she pretended that he was not talking to her, that he could not see her. But as I saw her glancing down at her worn gloves I knew that she knew he had seen her and that she felt naked.

Sitting in the waiting-room, with the pitiless spring sunlight illuminating the make-and-mend faces and clothes, listening to the ticking of the wall clock, I realised, without knowing why, that no shock or deprivation experienced inside the walls of the hostel could equal the subsequent dread of facing the hostile world outside.

The clock pointed to the half hour. A slow silent shuffle began towards the door. Bloody Mary was standing guard. The patient queue of women passed her. No word was spoken. They just handed in their discs.

I was the last in the queue.

'Your disc,' said Bloody Mary, barring my exit.

'I've already given it to you.'

'Your disc. Or you don't go out!'

'Look in your pocket,' I said.

As she pulled my yellow disc out of her overall pocket, two ten-shilling notes fell to the floor.

'Thank you,' I said, picking them up and offering her one, putting the other in my handbag.

'Give me that money!' she barked at me. 'Give me the money, or I'll call the Super.'

'Call the Super.'

'What is it, Mary?'

I looked round. Framed in an open doorway, at the back of the reception cubby-hole, was a calm grey-uniformed figure.

'A right twister this one is. Given me nothing but trouble from the minute she set foot in the door. Now she wants 'er money back!'

Like a capable hospital matron, the Super took the situation in at a glance and her voice was as calm as her face.

'A mix-up, eh? Well, that's what I'm here for.'

She gave me an understanding smile, then turned to Bloody Mary.

'Mary, I'll take care of the money for the time being.'

Bloody Mary had no option but to hand it over.

'You, my dear, had better come into my room and have a cup of coffee.'

'Thank you,' I said.

The curtains were still drawn. The only illumination in the room came from a lamp standing on a desk cluttered with the remains of a half-eaten breakfast and an ashtray overflowing with cigarette butts.

'Sit down over there on the couch, my dear,' said the Super. 'Relax and tell me what all the fuss was about.'

I told her.

'Let me see,' she replied, 'you slept here last night. No breakfast?'

I shook my head.

'Any extras?'

I smiled to myself, wondering if toilet duty came into this category.

'No, no extras,' I replied.

'Then all you owe is three and six.'

She rummaged in her handbag. I noticed how elegant her hands were. Beautifully manicured nails, a little long perhaps. She handed me my change.

'Don't hurry, my dear, you've been upset,' she smiled. 'I wouldn't like you to go away with bad memories. We do try to help people here, you know.' She offered me a cigarette and went over to a cabinet.

'What's your tipple? Sherry or gin?'

The incongruity of the uniformed figure poised over a cocktail cabinet, offering me gin at half past eight in the morning, was so absurd that I almost laughed. Instead, I pretended to be searching in my handbag for a handkerchief.

'Sherry,' I replied, looking at my handkerchief.

But it was not my handkerchief. The faint musky cologne was familiar. 'Rose Geranium' from Floris. And the initial R. 'Some people when they're broke go to Claridges, I go to Floris.' The tender ironic voice in my ear belonged to Robert. I put the handkerchief back in my bag. Like the woman in the waiting-room, I was trying to put away a memory.

The Super had switched on a portable radio. Wagner.

'Bung-ho!' she said, handing me half a tumbler of sherry.

'Bung-ho!' I said, taking a large gulp, hoping that the combination of my least favourite drink and least favourite composer would provide the inspiration I needed to get out of that suddenly oppressive den.

The Super came and sat down beside me on the couch.
'You've got troubles, haven't you?'
'Who hasn't?' I replied.
'Man trouble?'
I did not reply.

She moved closer to me and the wave of cheap scent and gin-laden breath made me feel sick.

'The two best cures for man trouble,' she tapped her glass. 'This and talking. Talk him right out of your system. Start by calling him names. Any name that comes into your head . . .'
'The Rock of Ages?' I said.
The Super choked on her gin.
'You're half-way cured already.'
She picked up my glass and held it to my lips.
'Now, a little drinkee . . .'
'No, thanks,' I said.
'Come on, a loving-cup'.

I turned away and was about to get up. But she put a restraining hand on my knee, and putting down the glass, whispered 'There are other ways of forgetting . . .' and kissed me full on the lips. The next moment her tongue was foraging in my mouth. I could make no sound, nor could I move. One strong arm pinioned me down on the couch, while the other fumbled up under my skirt and clawed at my thighs.

I tried to scream, but could not. Her tongue was filling my mouth. I did the only thing possible. I bit her tongue. Hard. As the blood spurted, she screamed with pain. In the struggle to free myself, I reached the edge of the couch. But her arm still held my thighs. I collected all the saliva I could, and spat in her face.

'You bloody cow!' she shouted.

I saw her face, blood and spittle oozing from her mouth, a clenched fist drawn back, then my jaw felt as if it had been broken. I heard the sound of the door being unlocked. I crawled towards it. A foot on my spine helped me out into the corridor.

G

I do not know how long I lay there before I heard a tapping noise coming down the stairs.

'Mother in Heaven,' I thought, 'Bloody Mary!'

But it was Peg-Leg. 'My Gawd!' was all she said. Somehow she supported me to the door. The bolts shot back. The door swung open to Peg's iron boot, and slammed behind us. We were out! Within minutes the fresh air began to clear my mind. I heard Peg-Leg chuckling beside me on the door-step.

'You do pick 'em, don't you!'

'The Super asked me in for a cup of coffee . . .' I began.

'And,' said Peg-Leg, 'like the lamb to the slaughter?'

I nodded, briefly telling her what had happened. 'She had just turned on the radio. And then . . .'

'And then?' Peg-Leg raised an ironic eyebrow. 'What did you expect from the Super? The Archers?'

Peg-Leg gave her leg-iron a final pat of approval.

'I must be off. Be all right now?'

I nodded. 'And thanks a lot,' I said.

'All part of the service.' Peg-Leg aimed a vicious kick at the front door. 'What was the name of the geezer who said we're all sisters under the skin?'

'Kipling,' I said.

Peg-Leg looked up at the 'Females only' legend and grinned her crooked grin. 'Never heard of him,' she said. 'But I'll bet he never kipped here!'

Chapter 9

The Garden of Eden

Blasted with sighs and surrounded by tears,
Hither I come to greet the Spring.

John Donne

As I peered at my reflection in my broken hand-mirror, I found myself looking at the face of a stranger. The thought of action was beyond me. Like a homing pigeon I had come back to the place that Robert had called 'our Garden of Eden', Battersea Pleasure Gardens.

For the moment I was content to look at green trees after the hideous hostel walls, to smell the newly-mown grass instead of carbolic, to watch the children playing in the sand-pit. The small painted doors on the Guinness clock burst open, and the Alice in Wonderland figures popped out as the musical clock began to chime twelve.

> But all the clocks in the City
> Began to whirr and chime . . .

Suddenly I was back on that New Year's Eve when Robert and I had climbed up the Tree Walk. I was half-way down the swing ladder, when I looked back to see if Robert was close behind me. He saw I was scared. 'Never look back!' he had joked. 'That way you fall downstairs!'

'Never look back.' But what else had I been doing these last two hours? What was there to look forward to? Another night at the Padlock and Chain? Suddenly I understood that I was in a situation which I had never faced before. It was a situation without hope, except perhaps one. The world of dispossessed women was unknown to me. Had I stumbled on an opportunity that in my professional life would be worth gold? Could I explore this world? Here, perhaps, was a way to become master, not victim, of my circumstances. Of course, I was only deluding myself. I was alone. I was broke. I was homeless. But I was not yet ready to face the full reality.

I looked in my handbag. I found my Post Office Savings Card, which I must have slipped in the previous day, meaning to cash it to help pay the rent. My present account stood at only twenty pounds, but that seemed life a life-saver. On my way to the nearest post office I made up my mind to spend five pounds on a style of living to which I would no longer be accustomed.

I had lunch at the Caprice restaurant, three tables from Zsa Zsa Gabor. Thawing out over *crêpes suzette* and coffee, I thought about my resolution to explore, research and report on the plight of homeless women. Mentally I began to draw up a curriculum vitae for my selection as a perfect candidate.

I began to think of where I might book in for the night. The YWCA came to mind. I did not know that I had picked on the Hilton of the hostel world and my fifteen pounds would soon be spent. But I was thinking of P and C standards and reckoned I would be able to live in a hostel long enough to do the groundwork of research.

'Did Madame enjoy her lunch?'

'Yes, memorable, thank you.'

But I could not remember what I had eaten. I fumbled for a ten-shilling note to leave as a tip, then started to get up. Suddenly, the whole room seemed to be revolving. I felt myself sway. Then I put my left foot forward. A violent stabbing pain struck my left knee. I heard myself scream. Then I blacked out.

Chapter 10

Cards to Newcastle

There is one Government Department which excels all others in the art of perceiving how not to do it. The Circumlocutionary Department.

Charles Dickens, 1869

Dickens's description holds good for the modern Welfare State. For three weeks since my black-out at the Caprice I had been going round in circles. Or rather, hopping around on crutches, with plaster up to my knee. St George's Hospital had diagnosed a torn ligament, suffered when I collided with the truck at the Elephant and Castle. My black-out and the pain were a delayed reaction.

I was broke, homeless, unemployed, and temporarily minus one good leg. For the first time, in a healthy, well-paid existence, I had to take a step which for millions of people is a part of everyday life. I had to make use of the services of the Welfare State.

For my first interview I reported to main office. I soon discovered that the London-based heart of the giant welfare honeycomb was too central, too easy to get at, and attracted more blow-flies than temporarily incapacitated workers.

In the company of about a hundred others, for three hours I had moved seat by seat nearer to the row of frosted-glass cubicles, issuing their relentless summons 'Next, please.' I had gained no help and two weeks later I paid my twenty-first visit, to yet another office.

It reminded me of early days as a RADA student. I had been fascinated then by the role of the prompter hidden away in the prompt box in the wings. One never saw him during the performance as he never left his box. One could only hear him and the rustling of his script or the occasional hiss of his voice when someone forgot his lines. I had forgotten mine in a scene from *Accent on Youth*. For my present debut I had no script. But if the behaviour of my fellow hopefuls and the atmosphere generated by the faceless ones inside their frosted-glass boxes was any guide, then my choice of script would have been *Accent on Kafka*!

'Get back in line, Mother Macrae! Or you'll wish you never left Killarney!' The whisky tenor tailed off into an apologetic whine. 'I didn't see you was a cripple. May God forgive me.'

'The top of the morning to you, Paddy! 'Ow's the Pope?'

A familiar whoop of laughter. A familiar tap-tap of an iron boot, as Peg-Leg sailed past, and disappeared behind Box Number One. This was the first time I had seen her since the Padlock and Chain. But, as I was to discover, the inmates of the hostel world are bound to meet, because of the limited world they share.

'Next week my foot! It's this week's rent I'm wanting,' Peg-Leg snorted.

With studied calm the promptress's voice from the cubicle was patient. 'I've already explained. We cannot supplement your rent without proof of address.'

Peg-Leg hooted with laughter. 'Put on your specs, Gran! Proof! It's written all over me, the Haven, Sally's Army, the Padlock and Chain; throw in Buckingham Palace for luck.'

'But,' replied the promptress, 'you're registered as NFA, no fixed abode.'

'Next please,' wavered the contralto voice of the promptress and, to cries of 'Hear, hear!' and 'Show a leg, Peg', Peg-Leg came out and began to sing in a high, twanging cockney voice:

> 'I've changed my abode
> Rather much of late,
> You'll find me at the Park,
> Third seat from the gate!'

This was obviously an old favourite with the hard core of the audience, who stamped and clapped in unison with the beat of Peg-Leg's iron heel.

'Next, please!' It was my turn. As I tucked my crutches awkwardly under one arm I tried to follow Sir Kenneth Barnes's advice to RADA pupils on how to cope with stage fright. 'Just before you go on the stage, don't think about your lines. Think about what you had for dinner last night and you'll feel so sick you won't care who is out front!'

But unlike in the theatre the prompt boxes presented an unexpected snag. Like pillar boxes or bird cages, once inside it was impossible to tell the front from the back. Propping my crutches against one side of the midget-sized cubicle, I squeezed myself clumsily into the hard chair.

'Good morning,' I said in my best RADA voice.

'Name, please?'

The voice came from behind my left ear. I tried to turn the chair round to face the voice, and knocked over my crutches, which crashed to the floor. I tittered nervously as I told her my name.

'Occupation, please?'

The voice was now coming from behind my right ear.

During the time spent on the floor trying to retrieve my crutches I managed to answer satisfactorily the string of questions, which ranged from hereditary disease to marital status. By now I had also got over my stage fright. After all, I had all the answers word-perfect, except the answer to the next question, which must be asked a thousand times a day.

'What is the nature of your inquiry?'

It sounds simple enough. But first you have to learn the jargon. Then, you have to keep clear-headed enough to answer it half a dozen times a day to half a dozen different clerks, who demand your answer signed and in triplicate. Then you come face to face with the fact that the clerks all suffer from the same disease : they pass you on to another department. Unemployment Benefit is sure that Sickness Benefit will fix you up. Sickness Benefit pass you on to Industrial Accidents. Industrial Accidents would be only too pleased to help, if only you had been driving that lorry, not merely run over by it. Try Unem-

ployment Benefit. On this occasion I was told that they wanted
to help, but they couldn't because my Insurance Card and
records had gone missing at headquarters.

Just where, I finally inquired, were the headquarters of the
Circumlocutionary Department located?

'In Newcastle.'

'Next, please!'

They might just as well have said Timbuktu.

Every moment of life good or bad, is worth remembering. But
I do not think I would have remembered much about the last
lap of my journey into limbo and my encounters with the Circumlocutionary Department had I not kept a diary. I had put
the initials DOQD on the fly-leaf standing for *Diary of Quiet
Desperation*.

My diary begins on the day I was carried out of the Caprice
restaurant on a stretcher and taken to St George's Hospital.

Day 1 : The medicos endeavoured to explain reasons for delayed symptoms. Detection and effect could take from 5
to 24 hours to appear. The recovery period, 6 weeks to 3
months.

I left hospital in plaster cast and on crutches and accepted
a lift home in an ambulance. Correction, I had no home to
go to.

'The YWCA', I said. 'And don't spare the horses!' It was
the same ambulance driver who had driven me to the Padlock
and Chain. Bert said he hadn't any girl friends at the YWCA,
which cheered me up considerably.

Arrived at YWCA. Bert wished me luck and as an after-
thought sent his love to Liz Taylor. I said I didn't get the joke.
He said I would when I got the bill.

Day 2 : Enforced rest at YWCA. Quite glad for chance to
put my feet up.

Days 3 and 4 : Ditto. Except no room to put feet up. Sharing
with two Christian Scientists and a Yoga practitioner.

Day 5 : (a.m.) Got the bill and Bert's joke. Left YWCA. Too
expensive. (p.m.) Two hours in phone boxes. No room at the

inn in Hostel Land. Finally settle for The Church Army. One single available at 22/6 per night. Breakfast 5/–, Lunch 6/6, Dinner 7/6.

Day 6 : Soul-saving matron summons me to her private altar. Perhaps she thinks I look like an atheist? Turns out she only thinks I look poor. Am I by any chance on NA? If so, will have to give up my private pew and join the larger congregation in the basement.

What's NA? A bogus religion or a drug? Oh, National Assistance. No, I'm not on it, I say, and I don't fancy it any more than I do segregated salvation!

Day 7 : (a.m.) Getting short of money. Left Church Army. No regrets. (p.m.) Afternoon in phone boxes. Reservation one night only. The Haven. A 60-bed dormitory, shades of the P and C. But instead of Bloody Mary, an ex-Roedean mistress. As kind as her cashmere and pearls are genuine. Insisted on lending me her best nightie. No strings. Just a boost to my leg-plaster-flaking morale. Happy contrast to Church Army and the P and C. Super!

Day 8 : (a.m.) Decided to continue investigating Unemployment Benefit. Trek to Circumlocutionary Office. (p.m.) Still investigating, Unemployment Department. Same old answers. 'Come back tomorrow.' 'Next, please.'

Day 9 : (a.m.) On the ninth day I rested on a bench in the park. (p.m.) Phone booth. Trek to Greycoats Hostel. In 100-bed dormitory. 8/6 per night, breakfast 2/6. Couldn't find a better hole, so book in for week.

Day 10 : Returned to Circumlocutionary Office No. 1. Reason for hold-up : no unemployment payments without proof of fully stamped card. 'Next, please.'

Day 11 : Trek to Circumlocutionary Office No. 2 (Health Department). I ask 'Am I eligible for Sickness Benefit?'

'No,' says the prompter. 'Being run over by a truck doesn't qualify you for any claim on this Department. Try the Department of Industrial Accidents.'

'Next, please.'

Day 12 : I try.

'Why didn't you apply to the Department of Sickness Benefit?' asked the prompter.

'I did. They referred me to you.'

'This is a borderline claim', said the prompter wearily. 'You are incapacitated from working as the result of an accident. But was it an industrial accident?'

'It was an industrial truck, Shell Oil Company.'

The prompter didn't get the joke. 'We shall have to get a ruling on this from Newcastle.'

'Next, please.'

Day 13 : Start off to revisit Circumlocutionary Office No. 1 (Unemployment Exchange). Yes, through the same door where I came in.

But Day 13 did not work out quite as planned.

I was again en route to Social Security HQ in Berwick Street; to reach it one has to cut through the heart-land of my profession, Wardour Street.

Someone once called Wardour Street 'the street of dreams which sometimes come true'. From the day when I first walked down the Street, carrying film cans under my arm as a bona fide member of John Grierson's documentary pioneers, the dream had become my way of life and had lasted over twenty years. Now it was my turn to walk down the street of broken dreams. But on Day 13 I just could not take it any more.

I stopped at a coffee-house and decided to check my progress as a voluntary pilgrim into the world of homeless women. The result was depressing. I had been spending three hours a day in one Circumlocutionary Department or another, two hours in one phone booth or another, two hours trekking from one point to another – and all leading nowhere.

I thought I was off course and in danger of losing my sense of direction again. But I was wrong. The vicious circle in which I found myself was the same circle, the same route, the same, well-worn one-way street, which the Peg-Legs and the Black Widows had travelled before me. My injured leg, my missing insurance card, my false pride and the ignorance which prevented me from getting help from National Assistance were only incidental factors, only relevant in that they had accelerated my progress to inevitable limbo. But I was too close to my subject, too involved, too confused to realise it at the time and over my coffee I was mentally writing off my investigation of homeless women as the failure of a mission. I told myself that I was too exhausted by my own day-to-day struggle for survival to observe and report on the living conditions of other unfortunate women. I still did not understand or admit that I myself was living in such conditions. And I did not foresee that before Day 13 was over I would have passed the point of no return.

I had just ordered another cup of coffee, which I could ill afford, when who should fall over my crutches and almost into my lap but an establishment officer from the BBC, whom I had privately christened 'Indeedy'. To be fair the only thing I had against him was his civil service jargon.

Picking himself up off the floor, Indeedy spluttered 'Fancy bumping into you. Long time no see. Yes, indeedy! How've we been keeping? Fit and well?'

'Apart from falling under the odd truck, fine and dandy, thank you!'

'Oh dear, we are in the wars, aren't we? Yes, indeedy. What is the nature of your injury?'

I shut my eyes. 'Indeedy' even spoke the same language as a circumlocutionary prompter. Perhaps that's what made me ask his assistance.

Indeedy listened patiently. The reasons for my plight were obviously no mystery to him. Nor was the solution.

'NAB will fix you up in a jiffy. Let me see now, I think I happen to have one of their forms in my brief case.'

'NAB? Translation, please.'

'Well,' he said, with an embarrassed cough, 'of course, it's not called that any more.'

'You mean the Social Services Department,' I retorted. 'I've already been round that circuit.'

'In view of your predicament, there is only one department that can supplement your requirements, the National Assistance Board. The nearest office is just behind Harrods.'

'Thanks, I can do without . . . that kind of assistance,' I said. I picked up the coffee bill and stalked out of the café with as much dignity as my crutches would permit.

Day 14 : Ended up sitting up all night on Waterloo Station. Hungry.

Day 15 : Raining. I slept on Charing Cross Station. Still hungry.

Day 16 : Booked in at Green Park. Third seat from the gate. Hungry.

Day 17 : Still at the park. Fourth seat from the gate. It had stopped raining and I stopped feeling hungry. I felt light-headed instead.

I recalled Indeedy's words : 'The nearest office is just behind Harrods.' I had never bothered to find out what was behind Harrods before. It is a short street. One-way. From where I was standing, trying to look nonchalant, the Harrods commissionaire asked if he should call a taxi. I thanked him, but declined. The commissionaire held up a Rolls-Royce as I hobbled across the street. In large letters, above the gothic doorway, was the legend 'National Assistance Board'.

'What is the nature of your inquiry ?'

My teeth were chattering with cold, but suddenly I felt feverish. For once I had an answer to their inevitable question.

I took a deep breath. 'I have come to ask for National Assistance. My National Insurance papers have been lost in Newcastle, but a friend tells me you can issue me with a temporary card.'

The clerk nodded and was already reaching for a form which he handed to me. 'Just fill that in.'

I obeyed. Indeedy had been right. It was easy once you knew the drill. The clerk scanned the form then handed it back to me.

'You have forgotten to fill in your present address.'

'I have no address at present . . .' I began.

The clerk's head jerked back. 'You mean you are NFA ?'

'NFA ?'

'No fixed abode,' he snapped.

No fixed abode ? Instead of remembering Peg-Leg and being able to laugh at the description, I suddenly felt humiliated.

'I have nowhere to live at the moment,' I said. 'I intend to get a room as soon as I have some funds, which I understand are due to me.'

I was copying Indeedy's words but I was frightened. The clerk snatched the form away from me. His whole attitude and tone of voice changed. I was listening once more to the monotone of official jargon. It always translated as 'No'. But this time it spelled out the Catch 22 of the limbo world. The authorities were not authorised to issue funds until I could give proof of a permanent address. The possibility of giving a false one was ruled out by the stipulation that one of their officers first had to call on you at the said address. After that, financial assistance would follow as night follows day. But no address, no assistance. My voice grew shrill as I protested that this was a chicken and egg situation. Before I could acquire a fixed abode I needed the money to put down for a room.

The clerk kept his cool. He had heard it all before. But rules were rules. Until I could give proof of address all he could offer me was a voucher for a hostel for one night. I would have to apply again tomorrow for another voucher, and so on. 'However there is one small payment I can give you,' he said, pushing some money across the counter. 'Ten and sixpence for daily expenses.'

I felt like an animal trapped on a treadmill. I could only nod my head when he asked if I wanted a hostel voucher. The clerk handed me a piece of paper. 'Here's the address.'

I did not look at it for fear it was the Padlock and Chain.

'Are you sure you're feeling all right?' asked the clerk with a glance at my crutches and plastered leg.

My head was spinning as I picked up the coins.

'Fine and dandy, thank you,' I said.

'Next, please.'

I got unsteadily to my feet. As I came out into the afternoon sunlight, both my legs felt like lead. I must get a taxi, I thought. But I had only the ten and six. I crossed the road to Harrods. But the commissionaire who two hours ago had stopped the traffic for me now just looked through me. He had seen me coming out of that gothic doorway.

Five minutes later, in the ladies lavatory in Sloane Square Station, I spent the first twopence of my 'National Assistance' being violently sick on a empty stomach.

Chapter 11

Limbo

Who's in the next room, who?

Thomas Hardy

I was unable to breathe and sweat was pouring down my face and arms. I was lying in a bed in a strange darkened room. 'Where am I?' I wondered. I turned my head and caught a glimpse of a little water-colour hanging above my bed. The picture kept expanding and contracting until eventually it came into focus. It was the perfect opening shot for a film. A scene straight from Constable's England. At the end of the day a farmer watered his tired horses in the village ford. In the background, framed in a bower of elms, stood a white-walled cottage. Through an open window there was a glimpse of a glowing fire and a table made ready for a meal. The farmer's wife, a child in her arms, was waiting in the porch to welcome her husband home.

Then the focus blurred. I tried to turn and face the voice which had come from behind my right ear. But I could not even lift my head from the pillow.

'Isn't it about time for another walk around the ward?'

The soft, calm, woman's voice was familiar. So was the face; so were the cool hands helping me up from the tangle of crutches and bed-screen.

'Come on, just once round the ward, then you can go back to sleep. It's either once round the ward or Guy's hospital for you, my girl. You can't laugh off pulmonary congestion.'

Every hour on the hour, I had obeyed her command. I had no option.

I thought of her as Girl Friday because it was on a Friday that I had collapsed into her arms, on the doorstep of the hostel to which the National Assistance Board had sent me.

But now it was Sunday, and I had had enough of being hauled out of bed and marched up and down like a helpless child. My protests were drowned when the coughing started again. When I stopped, perspiration ran down my face and arms like a shower bath. But I could breathe. The cotton wool which had been clogging my chest had been removed.

'Well done,' said Girl Friday.

For the first time I noticed the great blobs of cotton wool. Bright yellow cotton wool, clinging to the towel, the bedspread – everywhere, it seemed. A wave of nausea swept over me. I could still taste the rank yellow muck.

'Sorry about the mess,' I murmured.

'Don't be sorry. You've walked yourself right off the danger list. The patient will live. Don't you agree, Doctor?'

The doctor, a slim, smiling young man, agreed.

I murmured 'I don't think I've enough energy left to die.'

'Try sleeping,' said the doctor. 'This will help you on your way.' I felt a slight prick in my arm. 'By the way, congratulations. Doctors sometimes like being proved wrong, you know. But don't think the battle's over. You're on another kind of danger list now. We call it nervous exhaustion. There are only two cures. First, sleep. That's easy. Then guts. Not so easy. But the supervisor is better equipped to help in that department than any doctor. Don't worry if you have dreams or delirium, it's all part of the drill.'

The injection was already making me drowsy. Girl Friday was drawing the curtains and putting the screen back round my bed.

'Don't hide the picture,' I murmured. 'I want to dream of Constable's England.' Girl Friday laughed. 'I must pass that compliment on to the artist. Her name is Molly.'

'Molly,' I murmured. 'What does she call her picture?'

'I don't think she's given it a name, but ask her yourself when you meet her.'

I looked up again at the picture. I could almost imagine

myself walking up that garden path. The farmer's wife seemed
to be welcoming me home.

When I woke, I felt reborn. My body was rested and free
from pain. My brain, crystal clear. I did not know how long
I had been asleep. Nor had I yet discovered the name of this
sanctuary. But it did not matter. Through the drawn curtains,
a shaft of sunlight struck the side of the bed-screen. A distant
peal of church bells echoed through the window. I smiled to
myself. On this seventh day of the seventh week, thou shalt
sleep . . .

I was dozing off again when I heard a scratching sound outside the screen. Opening my eyes, I saw, through the folds of
the bed-screen, the flare of a match, followed by the glowing
tip of a cigarette.

'Why must they always follow me. Wherever I go, they
follow me, spy on me! Of course, I know the reason.' The
breathless husky voice broke off for a moment to relight the
cigarette. 'Can I help it if God gave me so beautiful a body?'
The voice suddenly became matter of fact. 'If this continues,
I shall have to complain to the Minister. Next time I catch
them spying on me with their beady little eyes, I'll know what
to do.' The voice was spitting with hate. 'Yes, I'll put out their
eyes. Burn their eyes out! Yes. Why haven't I thought of that
before? Burn their eyes out.'

I remembered the doctor's words. 'Don't worry if you have
dreams or delirium.'

But a smell of smouldering cloth made me look to the far
end of the bed where the burning tip of a cigarette was pressed
against the screen.

'Don't move.'

I had been reaching for my crutches. But the girl was too
quick for me. Through a gap in the screen, she was looking
down at me. I caught a glimpse of her face in the flame of a
match. It was beautiful. But it was the haunted beauty of a mad
Ophelia.

She smiled down at me and in that same matter-of-fact voice
said 'So you're not dead? Everyone's been talking about your
being at death's door for so long I believed them.'

Silently, she closed the bed-screen behind her and stood over me. In the dim light, I could see only her glowing cigarette.

'But I see their little game now. You're in league with the rest of them. A dirty rotten spy. I didn't spend years at the Foreign Office for nothing. I learned how to deal with people who play at being dead. As a matter of fact, I've just thought of the best way to deal with peeping toms.'

A speck of hot ash fell on my bare shoulder. I screamed. Within seconds several women rushed in and were wrestling with the girl.

'You stole my last smoke, you crazy cunt!' shouted one, as she tore the cigarette from her mouth. In a split second they were fighting.

Girl Friday rushed in and delivered a judo chop on their necks. She grabbed my visitor and bundled her out, shouting 'Do that once more and I'll burn your bloody paints and brushes!'

I fell back on my bed exhausted and trembling. Then, in the distance, I heard a faint, familiar sound.

Tap, tap, tap . . . Tap, tap, tap.

'Strike a light. Where's the bonfire?'

The screen was kicked aside, and Peg-Leg peered down at me. She took one whiff of the smoky air and choked. 'Mad Molly strikes again!'

'Did you say Molly?' I asked.

'Molly, Mad Moll. You do pick 'em don't you? She's usually kept down in the Casuals Ward, strapped to the bed. A regular nut case, if you ask me.'

'Why don't they have her certified?'

'Certified? You don't know Mad Moll. Every time they take her before the beak she fools 'em. Some soft old geezer takes one look at her, asks her something and she talks to him as sane as you and me. When he refuses to certify her, she hands him a parcel. He opens it. "Painted it myself, your Honour," says Molly, all sugar, "while I was waiting to be brought here. Please accept it." "It's beautiful," says the beak, "a peaceful English scene. It could not possibly have been painted by some-one demented. Thank you. This endorses my decision. Reminds me of a Constable." '

Peg-Leg grinned. 'Whoever heard of a copper painting

H

pictures! It's the same routine every time with Mad Moll. One beak fancied a cut off the joint. And he had it! Then he found out the truth. She never let him alone.' Peg grinned her crooked grin. 'They nearly had to certify him.'

'Peg, am I glad to see you! How the hell did you get in here?'

Peg grinned and aimed a savage kick at the fire bucket. 'The way I always get in. And I reckon I'll get out of this crazy world the same way.' She kicked aside the screen and, for the first time, I could see the rest of the ward.

'After the P and C this is a bleeding stately home. Rugs on the bloody floor, curtains, sheets on the beds. Even ruddy pictures on the walls!'

'What is this place called?' I asked.

'They ain't given it a name yet. Good or bad. But I can tell you what my old mum used to call it – "The Calaboose".'

'What's that?'

Peg-Leg grabbed one of my crutches and beat time with it, as she launched into one of her impromptu cabaret turns:

> 'In eleven more months
> And ten more days,
> I'll be out of the calaboose!
> In eleven more months
> And ten more days,
> They're going to turn me loose!'

'You mean this place was a prison?' I asked.

'Used to be the local pokey. My old mum used to book us in here regular, third cell from the left.'

'Peg, you're joking?'

Peg lifted the rug and thumped the stone floor with her iron boot.

'Once a prison, always a prison. It'd take more than a few frills and a picture of 'ome sweet 'ome on the wall to fool me.'

She spat on the stone floor, before kicking the rug back into place.

'What's more they 'aven't even changed the password. There's still only one way in and out of this place, the good old Padlock and Chain. You'll find out what old Peg says is true soon enough. Now it's time you had some shut-eye. Happy dreams m'lady.'

'Peg, before you go, there's just one thing I want. I want to see what's outside.'

'Stay where you are, kiddo. I can answer that one for you with me eyes shut.'

'But I want to see for myself. Help me to the window.'

'Oh, all right,' Peg muttered, giving me her arm. 'Some do like to do things the hard way.'

The small window with its bars was too high for me to see outside, so I climbed up on to a chair and, with Peg-Leg holding on to my legs, I looked out. Below was what had unquestionably once been a prison exercise yard. Deserted now. Dustbins standing like silent sentinels inside the spike-topped walls.

'Well?' asked Peg-Leg. 'Any wiser?'

'Yes,' I said. 'I've arrived.'

'Arrived? Where?'

'In limbo,' I said.

'Limbo? Sounds like some bleeding foreign country.'

'It is,' I said. 'A place where time stands still. The past doesn't matter, the present doesn't exist, and there's no future.'

'That's it!' shrieked Peg. 'You've hit the nail on the head.'

'What nail?' I asked.

'The name of this flipping place.'

Peg-Leg had forgotten me. She was acting a part, as she had done all her life.

'Just wait till I roll this off my tongue next time they ask me. "Your address please? No fixed abode, I suppose?" "You're wrong this time," I'll say. "And it ain't the third seat from the gate, neither. I reside at Limbo Hall." How do you like that, eh?' She hooted with laughter. 'Limbo Hall, that's my new address.'

Chapter 12

A Question of Survival

When sad, thou canst not sadder be,
Yea, in the night, my soul, my daughter
Cry, clinging heaven by the hems.

Francis Thompson

'Any woman subject to more than three nights' sleeping rough
is in danger of becoming a chronic case, a nomad for life.'

Girl Friday appeared to be examining her cigarette lighter
as if it was a new toy. But, as I had been acutely aware during
the past half-hour, the hazel eyes were watching me with the
close scrutiny of an examiner.

'Sleeping rough' conjured up a row of pathetic shapes
huddled on a station bench at midnight in full view of the
travelling public. I had once been one of the unwilling exhibits
but I had forgotten, until Girl Friday made me remember, the
night when in seeking shelter from the rain I had posed as a
bona fide traveller in Victoria Coach Station. I only tried it
once and felt so like a criminal that I was almost glad
when the police spotted me and moved me on before I could
dry out. One of the first things you learn about having no fixed
abode is to fear and even hate the police. They do not like
vagrants sleeping on their patch and they are constantly moving
you on, but I did not know I was committing a crime until one
night I was offered shelter in a police station. I was sleeping at
a hostel and in common with all hostels the house rule was that
you are turned out into the streets at eight in the morning
and the doors remain closed until six at night, when they are
opened for one hour only. Anyone missing the door even by

a few minutes is locked out. When I found I could not get in,
I sought help from the local police, who made an exception
and sheltered me because of my crutches and plaster, but told
me that being without a place to sleep is technically an offence.
When I arrived at the hostel at eight o'clock the next morning,
I was told I would not be let in until six in the evening.

'How many nights did you sleep rough?'

Girl Friday's question cut across my thoughts like an accusa-
tion.

'I don't know. I seem to have lost count.'

'Every woman says that, it's a danger signal.'

I flashed back at her. I was not every woman. And I had
only intended to sleep rough for a single night, as a last
resort.

'What about the second night, and the third?'

'What's this, the third degree? I tell you with me it was a
question of choice.'

She was waiting for me to go on, but suddenly my explanation seemed pointless. Until that moment I had still been
deluding myself that I was examining the landscape of the
dispossessed partly with the eyes of a film-maker. Limbo Hall
offered an ideal location and a ready-made cast. Now, at last
and quite suddenly, I realised that I was no longer directing
the action or shaping the drama. I had become my own raw
material.

'You were saying?'

'Sorry, I seem to have lost my train of thought.'

'You mentioned a question of choice?'

'Oh, yes. Well, at that stage I could only think of two, Green
Park or Black Rock.'

'You were thinking of suicide?'

'Perhaps. I hadn't the fare to Brighton, so I settled for Green
Park. There seemed to be no alternative.' My hands were shaking as I reached for my last cigarette. 'I suppose they all say
that?'

'You're damn right, they do. And with good reason! Nine
times out of ten there is no alternative.'

Girl Friday leaned forward to light my cigarette.

'But you timed things rather well. When you fell across our

threshold, the paint was hardly dry on the front door. Talking of paint, how do you like the colour scheme of my office?'

She patted the freshly painted iron bars across the narrow, uncurtained windows and held up two samples of material to the light.

'Which would you choose? The floral print or the grey stripe?'

'Oh,' I said, 'the grey stripe every time! It matches the view. You might call it Holloway Grey.'

'What shall we call this? Stick-in-the-mud brown?' She was laughing like a schoolgirl, and pointing to the still wet brown varnish on the skirting of the office floorboards.

I did not laugh back.

Girl Friday pulled up a chair on my side of the desk.

'I haven't had a chance to explain the object of this place yet, have I? It is to ensure that no woman need ever again be without a bed for the night. My first job is rather like Paul Revere. Only instead of a horse, I go out in the van. Every night from midnight to dawn, from Poplar to Putney, which reminds me . . .' She crossed to her side of the desk. 'I must make a note of that "third seat from the gate". Green Park, you said?'

'The tragedy is that for so many we're too late. They've given up hope, opted out for good. It happens so easily – overnight, like a fever germ.' She looked up at me. 'It's already begun to happen to you, if only you'd recognise the symptoms.'

'Thanks,' I said. 'I'd rather be infectious than felonious. The way you've been cross-examining me, one would think I'd committed a crime.'

'The only crime you might commit would be a crime against yourself – and that would be ever to do it again.'

'Sleep rough? Never! I'd do anything but that. Anything.'

'Anything? Then sign your name on this piece of paper enabling you to stay here for seven days, or at least until you are able to walk out on your own two feet. But first you will have to agree to stay here seven days as a voluntary prisoner.'

'A prisoner! Seven days! Just tell that foxy-faced gaoler downstairs to unlock the prison gates and watch me run out now!'

'You're my first disappointment of the day.' Girl Friday crumpled up the buff form, and threw it in the waste-paper basket.

'I suppose you can wait to say goodbye to the doctor? He'll be here in half an hour or so.'

'Not another half-minute!' I reached for my crutches. 'I know it sounds ungrateful, but I've a horror of being shut in. I always have had. The most terrifying memory of my childhood is being accidentally locked in a cupboard. As for agreeing to stay here as a voluntary prisoner . . . No, if that's what the doctor meant by guts, then he doesn't understand the meaning of claustrophobia.'

'He'd be the first to understand. He agrees with me that this seven-day rule is stupid . . .'

'Stupid? It's archaic! Peg-Leg was right. Once a prison, always a prison!'

An alarm-bell rang and a breathless warden, keys dangling at her side, burst into the room.

'Yes, Dorothy, what is it?' asked Girl Friday.

'It's Birdie, Ma'am, she's flown.'

'I suppose that was to be expected. Anything else?'

The warden flung down a small yellow disc on to the desk. 'Number Forty-one says she's leaving now. Won't even wait for her medical.'

'I suppose I expected that, too.' Girl Friday picked up the disc. 'At least she might have said goodbye.'

'She's in a terrible rush. Keeps carrying on about meeting her aunt.'

'Yes, I know all about that.' Girl Friday reached for a file marked 41 and began turning the pages. 'No other message?'

'Only to say she'll have you prosecuted for false pretences. Says she was hoodwinked into signing something she hadn't read. What's more, she wants her valuables back.'

'Oh yes, of course, she asked me to put them in the safe.'

Girl Friday unlocked the top drawer of a large iron cabinet beside her desk. It contained a collection of items resembling the wares of a pawn shop and a lost property office combined. The objects, all carefully labelled and numbered, ranged from miniature gin bottles to false teeth, 'falsies', family photos and the Pill.

Girl Friday closed the safe and opened a small shabby ring-box. Inside was an eternity ring, made up entirely of opals. This fact alone would have aroused my curiosity. Opals are my birthstone. But the fleur-de-lys design also invoked a memory of a person and a place.

For a moment I could not put a name to either. But I was certain that my encounter with the owner of that eternity ring had been of the same fleeting nature as my glimpse of the Black Widow at the Padlock and Chain.

'Well!' snorted the warden. 'That looks like the real thing! That's more than one can say for its owner or her auntie!' She mimicked an upper-class accent. ' "My auntie warned me never to sign anything without reading the small print." Small print! Anyone who can't read our rules wants their eyes tested or their neck stretched!' The warden chuckled 'That duty officer had the right idea, didn't he, Ma'am? Putting them regulations up so high on the wall no one sees 'em till it's too late!'

'That's a matter of opinion,' said Girl Friday sharply. 'Give Number Forty-one her ring. And tell the duty officer she's free to go.'

Girl Friday gave me a sad smile.

'My second disappointment today.' She reached for the folder. Then, abruptly, she picked up a pencil and wrote on the cover in large capitals 'Chronic Case'. Without looking up, she said :

'If you weren't in such a hurry, I'd tell you the story of Number Forty-one. You have a lot in common.'

'I don't know about that,' I said. But I had remembered. 'Though I think I know the story.'

And I told her of my brief encounter with the owner of the opal ring.

There were, in fact, two encounters. The first was on Waterloo station around midnight. She was sitting next to me on a station bench. Neither in appearance nor demeanour did she resemble the other regulars who sleep on railway stations. On that night I had believed her story about waiting for her aunt

who, having missed the midnight boat-train, would undoubtedly
arrive on the Calais–Dover connection next morning. Two
nights later, at about the same time, I overheard the same voice
repeating the same story. But this time it was Charing Cross
Station and the only variation of her explanation was her aunt's
itinerary.

She was so convincing that even as an eavesdropper I believed her that second night. So much so that I turned round to
see if it was the same woman. She stared right through me
without a hint of recognition. She was faceless as a ghost and
I would not have recognised her, but for two things : her eyes,
gazing emptily at the timetable of the Continental trains, and
the nervous gesture of the thin, worn hands, twisting and
turning her ring.

'So you noticed her eyes,' said Girl Friday.

'They will haunt me all my life.'

'They all get that look,' said Girl Friday, looking into my
own eyes. 'Even mere novices,' she smiled. 'It's all right. It's
quite gone now.'

'Thanks,' I said. 'Number Forty-one is just like all the others
– the Black Widows, even the Peg-Legs. Natural drop-outs,
proof of that old reactionary adage that the weak must go to
the wall.'

Girl Friday reached for my green discharge certificate.

'Won't you change your mind?'

'Sorry, I just want to get past those locked doors.'

'I've already broken one rule by not sending you to hospital. But if you walk out of here there's nowhere else you can
go.'

'Oh yes, there is !' I retorted, before I could stop myself.

'Of course, the third seat from the gate.'

'Aren't you being rather unfair?'

'Not half so unfair as you're being to yourself, or Number
Forty-one. You couldn't be more wrong about the weakest
going to the wall; so often it's the strongest. They rebel and,
like Number Forty-one, with good cause. That's how it starts.
But too often it ends up on a lonely railway bench.'

Girl Friday glanced at her watch. 'You'll have to excuse me.
Wednesday is my morning for Guy's. I'm late already.'

'Mustn't keep sick nomads waiting,' I said, wondering why I did not want her to go.

'Waiting is about the only thing they ever get used to,' commented Girl Friday, putting her papers in her brief case.

'I don't really blame any of you. The question of freedom is very much a personal thing.' She gave me a sad smile as she handed me my discharge certificate.

Girl Friday was on the point of putting the file marked 41 away in her filing cabinet. Then she took a paper out of it and handed it to me. It was an old tattered copy of the *Tatler*.

'While you're waiting for the doctor, take a look at the photograph on page sixty. I think you'll see what I mean about you and Number Forty-one having a lot more in common than sharing the same seat on a railway station.'

'Thanks,' I said.

Girl Friday gave me a quizzical look. 'You can wait here. I'll leave word for the doctor as soon as he arrives.'

Girl Friday paused in the doorway. 'And, contrary to regulations, I'm leaving the door unlocked.'

For a few minutes I sat looking at that open door. Then I took up the *Tatler* and turned to page sixty.

The face of a radiant young girl smiled up at me. She was wearing the ostrich feathers and white satin she had worn at her presentation at Court. Inset was a smaller photograph of the same girl, dressed in the uniform of the Red Cross.

As I looked more closely at that strong, determined face, her eyes held mine. They were not the eyes of a pathetic nomad waiting for a train that would never arrive, but the clear purposeful eyes of a rebel with a cause.

The caption read :

'Debutante of the year gives up season to volunteer for service as an ambulance driver with the Spanish International Brigade. According to latest reports, she is now serving in the front line at present under heavy aerial bombardment.'

Looking out of the barred window of Girl Friday's office, I recalled that as a teenager I too had wanted to serve the cause of the International Brigade.

Why then did I not get to Spain? Perhaps the reason was

simple – failure to follow through. Had this been a recurring
pattern in my life, paying lip-service to an ideal but never ful-
filling its demands?

I picked up my discharge card and was tearing it up when
I heard a sound behind me. Standing in the doorway, a bunch
of keys in one hand, a pair of shoes in the other, was the foxy-
faced duty officer. He gave me a yellow-toothed grin.

'Hear you're leaving us.'

He eyed the thin, torn slippers I'd been forced to wear since
my accident.

'Won't get far in those, will you? Better give 'em to me. I'll
put 'em in the dustbin.'

I handed them over.

'Try these for size,' he said.

I could see the clumping brogues were at least two sizes too
big, but I thought I had better accept them graciously.

'Thanks,' I said, as I tried them on. 'A perfect fit.'

'Always glad to oblige a new customer!'

There was a chuckle as the door closed softly. Then I heard
a key turning in the lock.

My first reaction was to beat on the door, or rush to the
barred window; to shout and scream for help. But I did neither.
I knew I had to control my panic. So I just sat where I was,
very still, looking down at the ridiculous great shoes and listening to the beating of my heart.

Outside, a clock began striking twelve. Girl Friday had said
the doctor would be there in half an hour. The clock was striking one when I finally got up, kicked off the shoes and began
walking up and down in my stockinged feet. Later that afternoon I learned how I had spent the two hours before Girl Friday
rescued me. I had passed out.

She told me that she herself had dispatched Foxy to find me
some shoes. She had asked him to tell me that the doctor was
delayed and that I was free to go or wait, as I chose. But Foxy
had chosen to lock me in.

I had not paced up and down the room, but round and round
the edge, like a wild animal in a cage. In doing so, I had walked
off most of the wet varnish and Girl Friday told me they had
to cut the stockings from my feet.

'As soon as you feel like it,' said Girl Friday quietly, 'you are free to leave.'

After a long pause, I heard myself saying 'I've decided to stay.'

'Under our conditions. It must be.'

'Yes. And what's more, I've even read the small print! Before I sign,' I said, 'can I choose my own disc number?'

'I think that might be arranged.' Girl Friday opened a drawer full of small coloured discs.

'What's your lucky number?'

'I seem to be fresh out of them,' I said.

Without another word, Girl Friday was already reaching for the disc of my choice as I said 'If it's going spare, may I have Number Forty-one?'

Chapter 13

A Hostel Day

*If I laugh at any mortal thing, 'tis that I
would not weep.*
> Lord Byron

'Wakey! Wakey!'
Was I having a nightmare? Or was that the voice of Bloody
Mary? This was my first morning as a voluntary resident of
Limbo Hall.
'Wakey, wakey! Rise and shine!'
No, not Bloody Mary, but next of kin.
I opened my eyes. The owner of the voice could have been
an over-made-up actress, an ageing *Mädchen* in uniform.
'Come on you! Shake a leg!'
The bedclothes were ripped off me.
I looked around me. It was hardly light in the ward. No one
else seemed to be shaking a leg.
'Mind if I get my crutches first?'
'Don't start pulling the old soldier on me, m'lady!' A grin,
full of bad teeth. 'Or should I say Princess?'
'Go it, Dot!' chortled a sleepy teenager in the next bed but
one. 'She'll find this a bit of a change from Buckingham Palace,
won't she, Dot?'
Girl Friday had told me that because I did not speak like
a refugee from *Coronation Street* one of the wardens had
dubbed me Mrs Armstrong-Jones. Now I knew which one.
'I'll show a leg when everyone else does,' I said, lying back
on my coverless bed.
'Out of bed this minute or I'll call the duty officer.'

'Go on, call the duty officer,' I said.

Without a word, the warden turned about and marched out of the ward.

'Now you're for it!' crowed the teenager, accompanied by a variety of cracks from the rest of the ward.

'Obey the rules, mate! Makes life easier. I should know. 'Ad going on thirty flaming years of it!'

The Cockney voice belonged to a woman with a face like a boot and the kindest eyes I had ever seen. Instinctively, in Louie I sensed a friend.

'Obey the rules, my foot!' The voice of Peg-Leg rang down the ward. 'If she comes near me, I'll put the boot in. Any road, it's still the middle of the flipping night!'

'Not night, mate.' Louie was peering through the curtains. 'Flaming dawn! Me mates are just beginning to pack it in.'

'Your mates?' I said.

'The stars.' Louie's weather-beaten face creased into a smile. 'Know 'em all by name, I do! Don't know what I'd do without me mates. They keep better time than all your flaming clocks.'

At this moment the warden returned with a sleepy young duty officer. Under his arm he carried what looked like a miniature sandwich-board.

'Understand you've refused to obey warden's orders. It is my duty to warn you of the penalties incurred for such conduct.'

He thrust the sandwich-board under my nose. Printed on it in large capital letters was the legend:

Anyone disobeying or otherwise abusing the authority of a warden renders herself liable to a fine not exceeding £35 or three months in prison.

I could not help it. I laughed.

'Since I don't happen to have thirty-five quid handy,' I said, putting out both wrists, 'I'll come quietly.'

The duty officer looked as if he might have laughed too, but for the presence of the warden.

' 'Old on a mo', 'andsome!' Louie flung an old dressing gown around her shoulders with a dignified flourish as if it had been

an opera cloak. 'Mind if I ask crab-face a question?' She
turned to the warden.

'We're supposed to get up at six, right?'

The warden nodded sullenly.

'And what time is it now, crab-face? 'Old on, I'll tell you!'

Louie peered through the curtains again.

'A quarter past five, give or take a few minutes.'

The duty officer took a quick look at his watch.

'Go on, 'andsome,' beamed Louie. 'Call me a liar!'

As red as a cooked crab, the warden was stuttering something
about having forgotten to wind her watch.

Louie had the last word. 'Your flaming kisser's enough to
stop Big Ben!'

The warden and the duty officer left to the accompaniment
of catcalls and elaborate yawns as the entire ward climbed
back into their beds with the exception of Peg-Leg, who proceeded to execute an iron-heeled jig and sang at the top of her
voice :

'Oh, how I hate to get up in the morning!
It's so much nicer to stay in bed!'

The floor show may have ended on a note of triumph for me
but it was a short-lived one. That morning I was put on toilet
duty and the warden kept me on TD for a week.

There is no sequel to my *Diary of Quiet Desperation*. The reason why I did not keep a diary at Limbo Hall was out of sheer
self-protection. Any diary of hostel life would be notable not
because of its contents, but because of its monotony. The daily
routine was always the same.

After being woken at 6 a.m. we had fifteen minutes to get to
the decent-sized, decently appointed wash-room, an exception
to the general rule among hostels. We were allowed half an
hour for washing and then from 6.45 until breakfast at 8 we
waited in the living-room. The decor was similar to the waiting-
room at the Padlock and Chain. There were windows on all
sides, but since it was four floors up at least the world could not

look in. Yet, curiously, very few women looked out. It was as if they felt it was not their world to look out on any more. The room was not big enough for the forty or fifty residents who had to use it. But it was the only room we could be in between 6.45 a.m. and lights out at 10 p.m. It was the dining-room, television-room and conversation-room for those who wanted to talk, but before breakfast no one did. We could see ourselves and our predicament mirrored in the person sitting opposite and we disliked what we saw.

At 8 a.m. two women would start hauling on the ropes that pulled up a dumb waiter full of plates and cutlery from the kitchen four floors below. Two others served the food, which consisted of porridge and cold spam. One egg per person was served on Saturdays. A communal tea urn contained a brew strong enough to trot a mouse on. After breakfast four women would wash the dishes, while the rest sat on hard chairs still trying not to look at each other. Those who had cigarettes smoked; those who had none, scrounged. Some talked of leaving that day or the next, of the job they hoped to get, or even of that jewel beyond price, a room of their own. Newcomers waited full of apprehension. Old-timers just waited.

At 9 a.m. the warden of the day allocated what work was to be done and by whom. The duties were performed between 9 and 11. As well as toilet duty, there was bed-making, dusting, polishing, carpet-beating, step-washing, window-washing. Kitchen work involved washing-up, emptying rubbish, and potato-peeling. The laundry was a basement kingdom all on its own. Sheets, pillow-cases, blankets, regulation pyjamas, were washed by machine and ironed by hand. I got through more sheets per hour than anyone else and was very unpopular as a result. I soon learned that many residents liked to spin out their duties as long as possible because they had nothing else to do to fill their day. Those who went out to work performed their duties before leaving or on their return.

Between noon and one o'clock the wardens, duty officers, Girl Friday, the medical officer and the rehousing officer combined their efforts to try to redirect those who had lost their sense of direction and to give hope where there seemed none. From the first-night casuals to the hardened regulars, all wanted another chance to live. But the odds were stacked against them.

At the bottom were the wardens. They were the link between the residents and the supervisor's office, providing verbal reports on the daily progress and behaviour of each individual under their charge. With a supervisor like Girl Friday these reports would go through the fine sieve of her own judgement, but with a less discerning supervisor the fate of any individual could lie in the hands of a vindictive or merely ignorant warden's report. Wardens determine the atmosphere of a hostel. For example, when the warden in charge follows it, the duty list is fair; but it can be altered so that those out of favour get the worst duties. Good wardens are difficult to recruit as the pay is poor, the hours long and the clientele rarely easy to handle or appreciative. At Limbo Hall their nickname was a wry comment on their functions and on the hall itself, for among us the wardens were known as 'settlers'.

Next in the hierarchy were the duty officers, usually men, who conducted their duties behind the glass doors of their cubicles below stairs. You only saw them when you broke the rules or when they paid out the weekly allowance.

The medical officer would see and examine every resident on arrival. After that he called twice a week and saw patients by rota or according to their needs. I was twice blessed in Limbo. There can only be one Girl Friday and one Doc. The first thing he said to me after I'd come off the sick list was 'The worst disease any of my Limbo Hall patients can suffer from is being here at all.' And the last thing he said when I was leaving was 'For every day you've spent here you've got to reckon on a month's recovery period. Settle for anything less and you'll come a cropper.'

The rehousing officer's job was vital since for eighty per cent of Limbo Hall residents the prime reason for their presence was a housing problem. His job was to find accommodation within the applicant's means, which were often limited since she might well be on National Assistance, while she found a job and reacclimatised herself to normal life.

Here was the real barrier for those who wanted to get out of Limbo Hall. Even if the rehousing officer was sure that the woman's appearance or background would overcome any prejudice, probably nine times out of ten he was wrong. The landlord would never say why, but as soon as he found out that her temporary address was Limbo Hall he did not want her and found an excuse to refuse her the lodging.

The rehousing officer could see the landlord in advance to ascertain any objections and to get, either by persuasion or legal insistence, an acceptance of his prospective tenant. But this could mean a worse experience than rejection. One girl who returned to Limbo Hall after living in a room obtained by the rehousing officer in this way told me 'Now I know what it must be like to be coloured.'

The rehousing officer compared his job unfavourably with a prison rehabilitation officer's : 'At least his flock have committed some crime against society, and, even if they've paid the penalty, you can't blame people, human nature being what it is, for treating one-time prisoners as suspect. But it's a terrible comment on our society if poverty and misfortune are to be looked on as crimes.'

The supervisor dealt with many aspects of her charges' lives. Girl Friday would overcome a landlord's prejudice, find jobs and combat employers' prejudice, mend marriages, save a girl from drug addiction or deal with the law, and everyone who left her office left it feeling less like a number and more like a human being.

To resume the timetable of a hostel day. Lunch was served at 1.15 and it was after clearing away lunch that the darkest hours began. I discovered this on my first working day. After washing up I lit the second cigarette of the day and asked the warden 'What do we do now?'

'Nothing.'

'I mean for the rest of the day,' I insisted.

'Nothing,' repeated the warden.

'But there's eight hours to go before lights out.'

'You get your tea at 5,' said the warden. 'Then you wash up. That takes an hour.'

'That still leaves seven hours,' I protested.

'After 7 you're allowed to look at TV until 9.'

Not only is the set on at full blast, but so is the conversation of those who watch. Eventually I got permission from Girl Friday to retire early to the ward.

'I think I'll take a walk round the block.'

'You need a pass,' declared the warden. 'Stamped when you go out and stamped when you come in by the duty officer.'

'Where is the duty officer?'

'Off duty, all afternoon.'

'I suppose you wouldn't happen to have seen the odd newspaper around anywhere?'

'If I had time to read newspapers, I wouldn't be doing this job.'

'Are there any books anywhere?'

'For them that wants to waste their time reading there's the public library.'

'Ta ever so.' I was on my feet again.

'You'll need a pass.'

'From whom?'

'From the supervisor.'

I sat down again. 'And she's off duty?'

'All afternoon,' said the warden.

That conversation took place on a Monday. It is equally relevant for every other day of the week except Sunday. On Sunday there is nothing all day. There are no duties, not even toilet duty.

In limbo time is your enemy. Anyone facing the empty hours of a hostel day must beware of self-pity. You have to find something to fill your mind. I think that subconsciously I was preparing this book and that saved me.

I once discussed the deadly boredom of the afternoons with a sympathetic warden. She told me the authorities were aware of its dangers. Originally the duties were scheduled to take up a full working day. But Limbo Hall, like all other hostels, was almost always overcrowded, so there was not enough work to go round.

I soon learned that exit passes were issued a week in advance for certain limited hours of the day and for specific stated reasons, a visit to hospital or an excursion to buy cigarettes. But on a weekly allowance of five shillings one soon ran out of reasons to ask for a pass at all. When I arrived, my allowance was only two and sixpence, because I could not do heavy work. I spent it on two packets of five Players and four newspapers. Soon I bought only a Sunday paper. The longer one stayed in Limbo Hall, the less relevant outside events seemed and newspapers even increased one's sense of isolation. Some spent their whole allowance on a visit to the local cinema. Others would eke it out on daily bus rides, or ride the underground for hours if it was raining. My haunt was the library. But for those who did not want or could not afford such activities there was nothing to fill the dragging hours.

Chapter 14

The Other Side of Eden

... when read or said
monochrome and grim
is dead and has, in fact
no gentler synonym.
                                    Vernon Scannell

To die in a hostel, any hostel, is strictly against regulations.
Death is not admitted, except by accident. Yet, within my first
week, death visited Limbo Hall in four different guises. As a
state of mind. As a gesture of despair. As a mortal sin. And,
lastly, in the shape of a mongrel bitch.

The state of mind was mine. My voluntary confinement
equalled voluntary death. The faces of my companions, the
calibre of my keepers, the taste of the food, the colour of the
weather outside, day and night, did not register. In retrospect
I can see that this hibernation was a way of protecting my
sanity. I had shrunk into my cocoon, waiting for that glorious
seventh morning when I could flee.

Yet, when it finally dawned, I did not even set foot outside
the door. During the briefing session in Girl Friday's office I
heard, but did not appreciate, the vaguely familiar words 'pass-
card . . . a bus ride . . . you won't get far on two and six.'

'Give this card to the duty officer downstairs. He'll let you
out.' The word 'out' jarred the ear-drums. I was about to experience my first encounter with the most common affliction of the
hostel inhabitant; that twin see-saw of insecurity, locked-in or

locked-out. I was now more afraid of being locked out. My pass-card in hand, I found myself, along with a group of listless, silent women, in the cramped basement waiting-room next to the duty officer's room. A green-painted wall clock was just moving to half past eight. Suddenly, from the pavement above us, a clatter of passing schoolboys blotted out the sunlight filtering through the basement railings.

'It was on this very spot,' announced a schoolmasterly voice, 'that Charles Dickens used to visit his father in a debtors' prison . . .'

'Blimey,' chimed a boy. 'Looks more like the Black Hole of Calcutta! What's that notice say?'

'Females only,' chortled a Cockney treble. 'Say Mister, you didn't tell us Dickens's old man was a woman!'

'And judging by the pong,' chimed a third kid, 'she's still down there.'

During this chatter I had shrunk back in my chair even though I knew that the passing pavement gapers could not see in. Then I recalled the waiting-room at the Padlock and Chain where the woman with the worn gloves looked out of a window through which the world could, and did, see in.

The door opened. It was Foxy. 'All right, ladies, all ready for the off. Mind your passes are ready for the Royal Enclosure!' A slow shuffle to the door. I did not move. I was remembering the reflection of fear in that woman's hand-mirror. Now I understood it.

Foxy grabbed hold of my disc chain as if I were a dog on the end of a lead, and with a quick flick of the wrist he slipped the metal disc under the collar of my blouse. 'Don't want the whole world to know our little secret, do we?' he said.

I wanted only to get as far away as I could from that open door and the sight, or sound, of the world that lay outside. I went back to the ward, although to be there during the day was against regulations. 'We don't want the whole world to know our little secret, do we?' I felt the whole world would know mine.

I ripped the chain from my neck. A minute later, I tried clumsily to join the broken links, as remorseful as if I had damaged a precious possession, which indeed it had become, the only clue left to my own identity.

That attitude would get me nowhere, except perhaps into a mental hospital. By coincidence, it was a kindred claustrophobic that came to my rescue, a mongrel bitch by the name of Faithful. Pressed against a hole in a suitcase under bed forty-two, next to mine, was her shiny black snout.

I untied the knots and a large shaggy dog leapt out, practically knocking me over. A moist tongue licked my face, neck and chest, slobbering with gratitude, or so I thought. Then I saw its face. I've never seen an uglier dog. It was slobbering and chewing gum at the same time.

'Hey pick-pocket! That's my gum!' I reached into the pocket of my blouse; the packet of biscuits was untouched. 'I'll swap you for some bickies.'

No sooner said than snatched.

'Hey!' I said, snatching them back. And, backing away from its slobbering jaws, in my best kennel-maid's voice I commanded 'Sit! Sit! and shake hands like a lady!'

To my surprise, the first part of my command was obeyed. But it was clear that the second instruction was beyond her capacity.

'Bad bitch!' I scolded, looking round for something to mop up the puddle. 'Bad dogs get no biscuits.'

The threat produced a heart-rending howl. Then we both heard the approaching step and jangling keys of one of our settlers. Before I could speak the shambling creature performed a backwards somersault that would have earned applause at a circus and was lying in the bottom of the suitcase, flattened from nose to stern, as motionless as a gun-dog in a game-covert. Only the brown eyes flickered, signalling an unmistakable command : 'Shut the lid, you silly bitch!'

I obeyed.

'What is the meaning of that hideous noise?'

'Noise?' Still on all fours, I asked 'What noise?'

'It sounded like a dog howling!'

'Oh, that,' I said, kicking the suitcase out of sight. 'That was me practising my impersonations.'

'Impersonations of what, pray?'

'Our dumb friends. Mad dogs happen to be one of my specialities.'

I made a go at foaming at the mouth, but the settler's eye had already spotted the puddle under my bed.

'And what is that? A part of the act?'

'Sometimes,' I said, 'one does get carried away by the part.'

'Hic!' A combination of chewing-gum and guilt was giving the dog an attack of hiccups.

'What's that suitcase doing under Number Forty-two's bed?'

'I don't know,' I replied truthfully.

'It's against regulations to leave luggage under the beds.'

'Perhaps,' I suggested, 'Number Forty-two left it there (hic) because she thought (hic) she might want to take something (hic) out of it (hic).'

'Something is going to be taken out of this ward instantly. You take one end . . .'

The alarm-bell rang.

'What's that?' asked the settler.

'You're new here?'

'Started yesterday.'

'Well, that was Tally Ho! Someone's got out. Go and join the pack.'

She ran.

I crossed to bed forty-two and kicked the suitcase. An angry growl came from it.

'Shut up you silly bitch. You were only saved by the bell. Now just play dead, while I go and find your mistress.'

The living-room at Limbo Hall was usually an overcrowded version of the waiting-room, the television providing the only sign of human animation. I had no idea what Number Forty-two looked like. But going on the principle that every dog looks like its owner and vice versa I soon spotted her.

Both she and Faithful had eyes that were a weak, watery brown. But when dog and mistress looked at each other, you knew at once that Mrs Brown was the born giver and Faithful the everlasting taker.

Come midnight in the Regulars Ward, all the women from sixteen to sixty were catering to Faithful's every whim and whine.

Thanks to the escapee – the uncageable Birdie, who was still at large – our settlers were closeted behind their own locked doors at a meeting, so the after-lights-out jamboree that followed was undisturbed by the usual hourly patrols.

Having downed a memorable dog's dinner smuggled from the kitchen and lockers in the shape of mints and other such precious items purchased with the frugal weekly allowance, Faithful was now being groomed. I noticed no appreciable difference between the 'before' and 'after' version of the faithless Faithful, but her mistress looked ten years younger and the regulars were having the time of their lives.

To a newcomer the presence of Faithful provided an unexpected and poignant example of the great deprivation that hostel life causes among women. It is not sex, although this is a loss that is felt from the moment any woman (regardless of how desirable she may have been, or may again be) steps inside the hostel world. What woman who performs her daily toilette in carbolic soap, sleeps in grey pyjamas laundered in carbolic, who is addressed not by name but by number, and whose only 'steady date' is cleaning the lavatories, could continue to feel herself an object of affection or desire?

But nothing can rob these women of their birthright to bestow upon others love and affection, or can stem their inborn yearning for an object on which to lavish these emotions. Faithful had somehow restored to them, if only for a few hours, their sense of womanhood. But with the sudden ringing of the duty officer's bell downstairs, signalling a new arrival, life abruptly returned to normal.

The new arrival was as usual admitted by torchlight and in silence. I was just drifting off to sleep, thinking that I might make use of that pass after all, if only to show Faithful what trees are for, when there was a rustling sound from the newly occupied bed on my right. Opening my eyes I saw in the moonlight the figure of a woman kneeling by the bed, praying out loud.

'Yea, though I walk through the valley of the shadow of death, I will fear no evil : for thou art with me, thy rod and thy staff they comfort me . . . I will dwell in the house of the Lord for ever.'

It was the Black Widow. I thought my journey into limbo had now come full circle. But I was wrong. I had yet to walk through the valley of death myself.

K

The next morning Faithful escaped.

Perhaps, in the dawn rush, Mrs Brown had not fastened the knots securely. Perhaps Faithful, for all her unendearing instincts, preferred liberty to prison. Limbo Hall seemed a strangely empty place without the homely touch she had brought and Mrs Brown could not be comforted.

Girl Friday put the official seal on the general feelings regarding the fate of Faithful. She was sure her nose would immediately lead her (if she did not hitch a lift in a police van) to that Valhalla of kennelless dogs, the Battersea Dogs' Home.

Mrs Brown was appalled at the thought.

'I don't mind being homeless myself,' she told me tearfully, 'but to think of Faithful rounded up with a lot of strays, and in a home for lost dogs. I can't bear it!'

But for seven days and seven nights Mrs Brown had to bear it. Her misery infected the whole place and was hard for us to bear too. She scarcely touched her food but, out of habit, smuggled bits and pieces into her handbag, only to realise when she got back to the ward that the suitcase under the bed was empty.

She hardly slept. Instead, she would sit beside the suitcase, rearranging Faithful's blanket, refilling her drinking bowl. Sometimes she would sit up all night, Faithful's string lead clasped in her hands, staring at the empty suitcase or opening and shutting it as if by some miracle, Faithful would reappear.

No one else in the ward was getting any sleep either, so Girl Friday gave out a nightly ration of sleeping pills, increasing the dose when they apparently had no effect on Mrs Brown.

But Mrs Brown had confided to me that she had never in her life so much as touched an aspirin and neither had Faithful. Once when she had been off-colour a vet had recommended some conditioning pills, but, as Mrs Brown proudly showed me, the box had remained untouched.

'Takes after her mistress does my Faithful. Wouldn't so much as look at 'em. I still keep the box as a reminder.'

It was not until that evening that I understood why she had confided this fact to me alone. Not wanting to hurt Girl Friday's feelings, Mrs Brown had been stashing away the sleeping pills in the pill box, and that night she gave me a knowing wink as she smuggled the box under Faithful's blanket.

Suddenly I had a feeling that we were being watched. I looked over my shoulder across the small aisle that separated the rows of beds. The Black Widow was gazing at me. But surely she neither saw nor heard anything except the ghost dressed in the First World War uniform?

The fifth day came and Mrs Brown, visibly pining away, still kept up her nightly vigil by the suitcase.

By the sixth day Girl Friday agreed that something must be done and let me put my pass to good use to go to the Battersea Dogs' Home to see if Faithful was there. She also told me to warn Mrs Brown that should Faithful be found she could not bring her back to Limbo Hall. She must find a home for her.

Practical as always, Girl Friday suggested phoning first to inquire about visiting hours. This proved to be wise since, had it been a Friday afternoon, the home would have been closed.

'What's behind all that waffle? Never on Friday afternoons?' I asked Girl Friday.

'Death,' she replied. 'A humane one, supervised by the Royal College of Veterinary Surgeons.'

I counted the number of days since Faithful escaped. Tomorrow, Friday, was the crucial day.

'Tomorrow,' I said, 'I'm taking Mrs Brown to Battersea. That's one reunion I wouldn't want to miss. It might,' I laughed, 'even make me cry!'

As a landmark in my mental geography Battersea Dogs' Home ranked alongside Grant's Tomb or Mount Everest. It was there. But the exact routes of approach remained hazy.

On Friday morning Mrs Brown and I set off. Girl Friday had provided the money to cover our journey. So I gave the bus conductress the exact fare without actually naming our destination. As the doctor had warned me, hostel neurosis like prison psychosis is quickly acquired and hard to shake off. This was my first day out. To ask, in front of a bus-load of respectable citizens, to be put off at a home for lost dogs would have been like asking a taxi-driver to drop us at the Padlock and Chain.

But as the bus rattled along by the Thames and Battersea

Power Station came into view, I began to feel uneasy. We were heading into the sentimental territory of Battersea Gardens.

'Excuse me,' I murmured to the conductress. 'Which is the stop for lost dogs?'

'Battersea Dogs' Home, ducks!' The conductress's lung-power matched her Tessie O'Shea proportions. 'Next stop but one, ducks.' She gave us a knowing look. 'You're one of them, aren't you? The minute you stepped on my bus I says to my-self "One of them!" It stuck out like a sore thumb.'

My disc was not showing. It was at the grieving face of Mrs Brown and at a brown paper parcel of tit-bits for Faithful that Tessie was looking.

'It was the look in your eyes, love.' Tessie's tone was almost tearful as she patted Mrs Brown on the shoulder. 'They all get that look, if you follow me.'

The whole bus was obviously following every word and I wished Tessie would stop.

'I know just what you're going through, ducks. I'll never forget the time I lost me little Flo. Never been through anything worse in my life. To my way of thinking my Flo was never lost. She was kidnapped by them vivisectionist brutes.'

The bus shuddered to a halt.

'This must be our stop.'

Firmly yanking Mrs Brown out of her trance, I led the way down the aisle of the crowded, suddenly hushed bus. Eyes were downcast or averted as we passed. But behind this silence and the averted faces, there was no contempt, disgust or pity, but sympathy and respect.

Tessie trumpeted after us. 'It's facing you, ducks. Just twenty yards up on the other side of the road. You can't miss it. When the wind's blowing right, you can hear 'em howling the other side of Battersea Bridge.'

I do not think I've ever been so glad to get off a bus in my life.

Comparisons can be odious but they can be instructive too, as I found when comparing the exterior view of Battersea Dogs' Home with the Padlock and Chain. No poison-ivy paint or cold stone, no bolted and chained doors, but a Swiss chalet perched on the side of the river Thames. Once inside the recep-tion hall, you feel you're a member of a unique club where you

need never feel alone if you have lost a dog. You will find your-
felt joining a queue, polite and orderly like all British queues,
but with the added hush that one associates with an accident or
a funeral.

During the half-hour's slow shuffle towards the reception
desk, I noticed that instead of dark dungeons there was an airy,
sunny lobby. Plaques on the walls bore names of eminent citizens proud to lend their names and give their money to the
cause of homeless dogs.

There were no rows of metal discs and keys. There were no
regulations hidden away in a dark corner.

'Next please!'

The voice belonged to a pert, pekinese-faced blonde behind
the reception desk. She asked one simple question : 'Are you
visiting or looking for a lost dog?'

A nod to the latter category. We were handed a green form,
free of circumlocutionary jargon. The instructions might have
been penned by Beatrix Potter. 'Will the owner of a lost dog
kindly hold this form in the right hand and wait by the tree
until the keeper arrives.'

We went through some glass swing-doors out in to a pocket-
sized exercise yard dotted with large signposts. An arrow pointed
to the entrance of a dark, cool, carbolic-smelling corridor. Did
it lead to the place that Girl Friday had in mind when she
talked of 'a humane death'? I had a sickening feeling that it did
and quickly turned away.

Emerging into the blazing sunlight, I spotted Mrs Brown
disappearing under another archway sign-posted 'Lost dogs'.

'You must obey the regulations,' I said. 'It says here "Wait
under the tree". But where on earth is it?'

Then I spotted it. The smallest tree that was ever nurtured
in Battersea soot. A train thundered directly above our heads.

When the smoke cleared, my heart gave a lurch. Beyond
the railway bridge, silhouetted in the distance against the cloud-
less summer sky, were the gay towers of Battersea Pleasure
Gardens and the green haze of the Tree Walk. I had stumbled
on the other side of Eden.

'Breed? Bitch? Dog? Name?' we were asked by a wizened
little man, dressed in the white coat and peaked cap of a keeper.

'Mongrel,' I replied. 'Bitch. Sometimes answers to the name of Faithful.'

The keeper led us under the arch of the railway bridge, up a short flight of stone steps and on to a sort of circular rostrum. About a dozen lost dog owners were pressing their faces against a wire netting screen, gesticulating wildly.

'Mitzie! There she is! Mitzie!'

The joyous yelp belonged to a woman who had done us out of our turn in the queue at the reception desk. Now she was doing the same with our share of the view through the wire netting. Above the canine cries rose the voice of the dog-catcher.

'Is this your Mitzie, lady?'

A fat hand, loaded with rings, jabbed through the wire netting.

'Right! A poodle. Now then move along, please, lady,' the keeper barked. 'Your dog will be awaiting collection at reception.'

'Come along, my dear!' called her long-suffering husband. 'Mustn't keep Mitzie waiting.'

She was fumbling in her crocodile handbag. With a flutter, she produced a ten-shilling note.

'That's for you.'

'Thank you, madam.' The keeper suddenly acquired stature. 'But we don't accept tips from customers.'

Even inside her mink stole, she froze.

I gently nudged Mrs Brown forward. But she hung back. A mute appeal in her eyes said 'Look first, just in case.' I saw a yelping, sprawling mass, like a huge gyrating dog-skin rug. Wagging tails and beseeching eyes added up to one single-throated agonised appeal: 'Get us out of here!'

But the plea was not quite unanimous. One dissenter had spotted something of greater interest than the sight of a familiar face. Faithful, with her face buried in the communal food-trough, was hogging the grub while the other dogs' backs were turned.

Gently, I pulled Mrs Brown forward.

'There she is,' I said. 'I told you Faithful had more lives than a cat! Finding her was easy. But finding someone to take her away, and give her a home . . .'

'Take my Faithful?' broke in Mrs Brown. 'No one's going to take my Faithful away from me, no one!'

I started to explain Girl Friday's warning about the hostel regulations that did not allow dogs to live there.

But Mrs Brown seemed not to be listening. She was gazing down through the netting and, when she found her voice, it was more like a sob.

'Faithful! Faithful!'

'Speak up, missus!' called the keeper. 'Is this your Faithful?'

But Mrs Brown was now beyond speech. Tears were pouring down her cheeks. Then, to my bewilderment, in answer to the keeper's question, I saw she was shaking her head.

'Come on, lady,' said the keeper. 'Is this your Faithful or isn't it?'

The look in Mrs Brown's eyes was answer enough.

'Well then, now everybody's happy!' The keeper came out and patted Mrs Brown's arm. He actually seemed happy himself.

'Now then, go to reception and you can take your Faithful back to "Home Sweet Home".'

Mrs Brown looked down once more through the wire netting. A long, lingering look. Then she said to the keeper in a loud clear voice 'That's not my Faithful.'

I was dumbfounded and I took her arm. 'Why did you say that? What's wrong?' The look in her eyes said it all. I did not try to stop her as she walked slowly down the stone steps under the archway and out of sight.

'Could I have a word with you?' I asked the keeper. The perpetual background of the barking made it difficult to tell him Mrs Brown's story.

The keeper showed neither sympathy nor shock. Homeless women were outside the rules and regulations of his little kingdom. But homeless dogs were a different matter. Faithful's lease of life under that status probably had only a few more hours to run.

There were only two possibilities, I was told, of prolonging that lease. An offer of adoption or a reserve. This amounted to a down-payment to cover Faithful's board for one week.

'How much is the reserve?' I asked.

'Minimum of two pounds,' murmured the keeper. He might as well have said two hundred.

'Look,' I said, 'I might be able to make some arrangement. But I need time. What's the deadline?'

'Three o'clock this afternoon.'

Almost on cue I heard a clock striking two.

'I don't know how I'm going to tell Mrs Brown,' I said to the keeper, who suddenly took off his cap. I looked up. Standing beside us, dry-eyed and composed, was Mrs Brown.

'It's time we was getting back,' she said, and silently she turned and walked away.

I followed her past the sad, sooty little tree. She did not look back, not once.

When we reached the entrance hall, Mrs Brown paused by the donations box.

'Why did you say it wasn't Faithful?' I asked.

' "Home Sweet Home," the keeper said, you heard him. That's where Faithful belongs. But where's my home?'

'You realise what will happen this afternoon if . . .'

'Yes,' said Mrs Brown.

'Look,' I said. 'There must be some way.'

'No,' said Mrs Brown. 'She'd be better off dead. Much better off.' That mute look in her eyes told me she was speaking not only of Faithful.

She stopped by the collection box, opened her shabby handbag, and dropped some change into the box.

Tessie was right. We could still hear them howling as we started to walk across Battersea Bridge. No, I had not lost my sense of direction. I just could not take Mrs Brown back to face that empty suitcase. Not yet. And I was not sure I could face it myself.

Anyway, I still clung to one last hope. I would phone Girl Friday. She might come up with a solution. But she was off duty until three o'clock.

In the meantime there was time to kill. I headed back to the one place where in my memory time stood still. The Garden of Eden. It was a bad trip to Paradise.

Mrs Brown seemed to have lost not only her power of speech, but her will to live.

It was not three o'clock yet, but I could not wait that long.
There was always someone on duty. The nearest phone box
was across Battersea Bridge. Ten minutes' walk, there and back.
'I'll be back inside twenty minutes. Will you be all right?'
Mrs Brown nodded and continued to stare at a pleasure
steamer cruising down the Thames. I had an uneasy feeling
that if I had said I would be back inside twenty years Mrs
Brown would have nodded just the same.
'You've had nothing to eat all day. Can I bring you back
a sandwich?'
Mrs Brown shook her head. Her brown eyes were looking at
me, the way she used to look at Faithful.
'You're the one who could do with a sandwich. You look
worn out.'
'No, I couldn't eat it. Anyway, I have no money.'
Mrs Brown took off her gloves and opened her purse.
'No,' I protested, 'I was only joking.'
'Please,' said the ever-lasting giver, pressing some coins in my
hand. 'Just to please me.'
So I left her, sitting primly on the gaily painted seat over-
looking the Thames, which reflected the radiance of the sum-
mer afternoon.
As I reached the exit I stopped and looked back. But Mrs
Brown did not see me wave. She had finally opened the paper
bag and was feeding Faithful's scraps to a pair of swans float-
ing past on the river below. For once at least in her lifetime
Mrs Brown's offering was received with the grace with which
it had been given.
The phone box by Battersea Bridge was out of order.
It was in Tite Street, two doors away from the flat where
Robert and I had lived, that I finally found a phone box and
dialled the number of the Samaritans. It was by no means the
first time I had dialled that number. Long ago I had spent
three months preparing a film about the Samaritans.
For what seemed an eternity no one answered, then suddenly I heard a voice saying 'The Samaritans here. My name
is Patricia. I don't want to know your name. I only want to
know how we can help you?'
After I had told her the details she said that a member of

the Samaritans Mobile Unit would be there within half an hour.

The Samaritans, as always, kept their appointment to the minute. But that was exactly thirty minutes too late. The clocks along the river were tolling the hour, like an echoing benediction, as I stood watching the small black police launch slowly returning to the pier bearing Mrs Brown's body. I could not pretend to hope that the woman who had spent the last half-hour of her life feeding the swans on the banks of the Garden of Eden would have remembered it as such. But I was fairly certain that she would neither expect nor wish to come any closer to paradise than to be as near as she could to Faithful in what was probably the final hour of life for both of them.

It was long past lights out when I finally returned to Limbo Hall.

According to Foxy's interpretation of the regulations, as the office safe was locked, there was no 'receptacle wherein to lodge the deceased's effects'.

'Nothing in it of any value, is there?' asked Foxy, opening Mrs Brown's shabby handbag.

'No,' I said. 'She gave me the last penny she had in the world.'

For the first time I realised the exact moment that Mrs Brown had reached her decision. The coins she had pressed into my hand amounted to one and ninepence, her bus fare back to Limbo Hall.

'Well,' said Foxy, with a try at a grin, 'put it in the kennel, with the rest of Number Forty-two's belongings.'

So the last thing I did that night was to lodge her handbag in the empty suitcase under bed number forty-two. Turning away from the empty bed next to mine, I closed my eyes.

'Yea, though I walk through the valley of the shadow of death . . . I will fear no evil, for thou art my rod and my staff.'

Had I not known otherwise, the voice of the veiled figure in black kneeling by the next bed could have belonged to a young girl.

'Oh, nark it!' yawned a voice from the other end of the ward.

'Leave the poor soul in peace!' cried out a second.

'Thank Gawd tomorrow's 'er seventh day, and Sunday, too! She'll be getting up bright and early and off to a proper Mass!'

But the Black Widow did not get up bright and early. She had attended her last Mass, at her own altar.

When the warden found her in the morning, clasped in her folded hands were three items : her identity disc, a rosary, and the faded photograph of a young man dressed in First World War uniform. On the floor, close to where she had knelt for her final confession, was Mrs Brown's little box containing the sleeping pills. It was empty.

It was my turn on the next morning's duty rota to make the beds including the two on either side of my own. A complete strip down to blankets and mattress. I set about the task with as much emotion as a chambermaid. Yesterday, the occupants of these two empty beds had been alive. Today they were dead. Yet to me those two empty beds were just numbers. Forty and forty-two – a complete strip.

'Which is number forty-two?'

I looked up. The voice belonged to a young girl with the face of a Botticelli cherub and the body of a Delilah.

I indicated the bed newly vacated by the Black Widow. The cherub tried it for size.

'Smells of carbolic, don't it?'

'Yes,' I said. 'It smells of carbolic.'

'They said number forty was going spare,' the cherub was eyeing the freshly plumped up pillow on which Mrs Brown had hardly laid her head.

'Take your pick,' I said. 'They all smell of carbolic.'

'Straight up?'

I looked up. A completely nude Delilah.

Leaving her fragile briefs lying on the floor like a swimmer discarding a towel on the beach, she plunged under the cover of the grey blankets of bed forty.

A minute later, the face of the cherub and the outsized breasts of Delilah re-emerged over the top of the blankets.

'The name's Marina. No relation to the princess. What's yours?'

'We go by numbers here,' I said.

'What about that number down in the front office? Smells lovely, she does. Chanel No. 5.'

'She runs the place,' I told her.

'Straight up? Is she a les?'

'I don't know. I haven't asked her. Why?'

The cherub was idly cupping her breasts, which protruded above the blankets.

'Just want to get on her right side. Les's are easy. One look at these and they foam at the mouth. One touch of 'em and they're a pushover. I've got to get out of here on Saturday.'

'Saturday is step-washing day,' I said. 'No passes on Saturdays.'

'Straight up?'

'Straight up,' I replied.

'I've got to! It's the only day to see my brother.'

'Where's he?'

'Borstal.'

'Borstal?'

'They caught him doing me. Been doing me for years, he has. But this time they caught him.'

I tried not to look surprised.

'And . . . what did you get?'

'Remand home, but there weren't any vacancies. So here I am, ready and willing. You miss it after getting it regular, don't you? Say, where do you go up here, when you want to?'

'You don't,' I said, 'It's down five flights.'

'Straight up?'

'Straight up, down, or sideways.'

'You're a comic. What you say your name was?'

'I didn't.'

The face and breasts disappeared under the grey blankets. A minute later, the cherub's nose appeared, sniffing the air like a Bisto kid.

'Ooh, carbolic. Luverly!'

I shall always remember Marina for that. She made me laugh when I was nearer tears than I had ever been in limbo.

Chapter 15

The Net

The Social Security System, which is an integral part of the Welfare State, spreads its safety-net beneath most, but not all of its citizens. Those who fall through the meshes are often victims of ignorance as to their rights or pride which forbids them to accept what is theirs by right.

Pauline Geest, *The Welfare State*

It always happens on Saturday in any hostel. Saturday is 'over the wall day'. I chose the Saturday that followed the deaths of Mrs Brown and the Black Widow.

I had to get out and away. But how? Even the humblest escape needs finance. Since my unwillingly given signature on the dotted line of the National Assistance form had got me into Limbo Hall, I assumed it would also get me out.

I needed enough money to put down a week's rent in advance to obtain a room of my own, which is what I needed most. I had not forgotten Catch 22. 'No fixed abode, no funds.' But, I reasoned that over six months' residence at Limbo Hall would fulfil that requirement.

I became obsessed with my plan. I did not confide in Girl Friday. Partly because it seemed like ingratitude to be so anxious to get away from her, but chiefly because I was not sure of my chances of success.

Armed with three and sixpence hoarded from the Friday allowances and a pass obtained for 'a visit to the library', I boarded a bus.

My first stop was St George's Hospital, where despite medical protests I had the cast removed from my leg and shed my crutches. I felt almost well-dressed without them.

My next stop was a fivepenny bus ride away to that gothic archway behind Harrods.

I had made my first big mistake. You cannot claim any assistance except from the NAB office in the district where you slept the previous night.

Half an hour later I found myself sitting in an office I had never visited before, which provided a view through the window of Limbo Hall.

Secretly hoping that my initiative would earn some applause, I explained that I wanted assistance in order to leave Limbo Hall.

For the first time I was slap up against what the doctor was later to describe as 'the graduation from the Welfare safety net into the path of no return'. The psychological and practical effects of being caught inside the Welfare net are that the dispossessed female finds herself encircled by a red-tape jungle, which not only hinders her efforts to rehabilitate herself in society but seems actually to discourage her from trying to do so.

This was now expressed to me by the NAB clerks. They were surprised that anyone should wish to graduate from their hostel, aggrieved that their largesse had fallen into rebel hands, and indifferent because they knew that in nine cases out of ten the rebel will get no further than I would in my bid for freedom since they control the supply of money.

The clerk treated me with the silent contempt reserved for rebels and slowly, and reluctantly, counted out £2 13s 11d. How he reached this figure, I did not ask. But I did venture the opinion that, while the payment might just cover phone calls, fares and a sandwich, even if I was hiking fit, it would not find me a room demanding a week's rent in advance by nightfall.

The official replied 'That's all you're getting. And it's no concern of ours where it gets you.'

My escape had lasted just under three hours, during which time I was never further than a shilling bus ride away from Limbo Hall, to which I returned, defeated.

During my time at Limbo Hall fifty per cent of the women who passed through were transitory – temporary victims of some financial or domestic crisis, staying only one or two nights, probably never to return to a hostel again in their lives. Fifteen per cent were regulars, like Peg-Leg and the other Number Forty-one, fated to live out their lives in Limbo. The remaining twenty per cent were, like myself, aspiring graduates.

The first step to graduation is to get a job, which is never an easy step for anyone caught in the bottom of the net. For various reasons, I was one of the last of that year's crop to fight my way out to employment.

Within a week of my attempted escape I burst into Girl Friday's office, outraged because she had not yet found me the promised job. I interrupted a farewell interview with a girl who had occupied bed thirty-two and was delighted to be returning to her old job. She was a bed-maker. Girl Friday's comment on my attempt to compare my failure with her success was brief, but to the point.

'Once a bed-maker, always a bed-maker. Remember telling me about a television producer being as good as last night's programme. How long ago is it since your last programme?'

'So long,' I said, 'that I don't suppose anyone even remembers how bad it was . . . *Lost without Trace*. A prophetic title! But I'm not aspiring to a come-back, I just want a job . . . any job.'

'Any job?' Girl Friday raised a quizzical eyebrow. 'You have to go easy on that leg for the next month or so, which rules out ninety-nine per cent of the employment market at our level.' She picked up a copy of *The Times*.

'But there was something in the Personal Column today that made me think of you. Didn't you tell me that you once sold space over the telephone?'

The thought of the Grub Street jungle made me shrink back in my chair. Suddenly I was aware of the truth in the doctor's warning about the psychological effect of hostel life. He illustrated his point with the story of a seventeen-year-old boy and his reply to a welfare officer, who had been trying to persuade him to accept a voucher to spent a few nights in a Salvation Army hostel.

'Not on your Nelly. I'd rather go back to quod!' answered the boy.

'What you lack is character,' rebuked the welfare officer. 'It takes a good strong character to get into a Salvation Army hostel.'

'What you mean,' retorted the boy, 'is that it takes a fucking sight stronger character to get out.'

I probably had an easier struggle than some to escape from limbo. But I doubt whether I would have managed it when I did if it had not been for an accident.

My first job was to be an egg-breaker in a near-by factory and my co-worker on the conveyor belt was Marina. At the end of the week Marina decided to break the monotony. She put her egg-belt into reverse, stepped on the gas, and a week's output of the Light Sussex, Buff Orpington Section, disintegrated into scrambled eggs. I did not laugh. I was too busy doing some rapid calculations on my financial position.

I decided there must be a quicker way to earn enough money to enable me to pay the £4 10s 0d rent to Limbo Hall (always deducted from wages) and still have enough left over to put down a deposit on a room of my own.

So I took a job as a dish-washer in the canteen of a newspaper printing works. I earned two and sixpence an hour plus a free daily pinta and a free daily newspaper. The prospects looked better, sixpence an hour more than my last job and two shifts instead of one, so I signed on for dawn duty – when a fleet of yellow vans roar out of the staff gateway with the speed and urgency of a military convoy to deliver bundles of newspapers fresh off the press.

In the canteen that morning I spotted a familiar face among the gang queueing up for early breakfast. He had spotted me too, though much to my relief he hadn't recognised me.

'This is not your line is it, washing dishes? I'm a reporter. Normal occupation TV critic. Right now I'm conducting a survey on public opinion, individual reactions to changes in TV programmes over the past five years. A sort of one-man TAM. Now, in that time, what would be the most memorable programme you've ever seen?'

'I forget,' I said truthfully.

'Thanks.' He started scribbling something in his notebook. 'May I quote you? Perfect punch-line for my article. I'm thinking of calling it "All our TV Yesterdays". No, that's been used. How about "Lost Without Trace"? Hey, where are you off to?' The last person I wanted to talk to was a TV columnist who had given my BBC programmes many a good notice.

I changed my job as a result of this encounter and was now in a skyscraper block containing the executive offices of Britain's largest paper manufacturers. My remuneration was two pounds a day for a five-day week. Even allowing for the deduction for my bed and board at Limbo Hall, I would with luck have enough money to acquire a room within perhaps two months.

It was four o'clock in the afternoon. Seventy-three trays and one hundred and ninety-three cups and saucers had been collected and conveyed along the highly polished corridors thanks to the joint efforts of myself and Tilly, a nickname I had given to the one-ton unsteerable aluminium tea-trolley. But that afternoon even the truculent Tilly seemed to be gliding along on greased axles. One second I was carrying a tea-tray, the next I was skating, then tobogganing along the floor on my bottom. Something green loomed up in front of me. I stretched out my arm. I remember hearing a sound like the snapping of a twig as my wrist collided with the sharp edge of a metal filing cabinet.

There was no pain. Not yet. I was sitting on the floor, looking at the bone bulging out at right angles from my wrist.

'Has the last cup of tea been served?' asked the supervisor.

'Yes,' I replied, looking at the broken crockery. 'And cleared away.'

I handed him the empty tea-tray, which I still held in my good hand, and fainted.

Four hours later, my left arm in a sling in preparation for the plaster which was to be put on the following day, I returned to Limbo Hall in the manner to which I was becoming all too painfully accustomed. I even had the same ambulance driver. Bert had changed hospitals and ambulances since we last met, but his laconic philosophy remained unchanged. All the comfort Bert had to offer this time was 'Good job it wasn't your right arm.'

L

It was the doctor who broke the good news to me.

'You are in luck. You are now eligible for injury payment,' he told me. 'All of seven pounds a week and payable throughout your incapacity, which will be at least three months.'

'I don't call three months at Limbo Hall good luck,' I said, 'considering they will take the bulk of the money for board and lodging.'

'They won't take a penny. They can't,' he replied. 'Unlike any money you earn, the disability payment is all yours. In a few weeks you'll be able to put down a payment on that room of your own you want so much.'

My fellow inmates treated me either as a heroine or a fraud. It was Candy, a tough fifty-year-old Australian woman, who gave me my first clue. When I first came back from the hospital with my arm only in a sling, she looked with suspicious eyes at my arm. 'Broken is it? Who do you think you're kidding!'

She plucked at my arm and pulled it out of the sling. I screamed at the pain.

'Sorry, cobber,' she said, 'I thought you were skiving.'

Puzzled, I related the incident to Peg-Leg.

'You're still green behind the ears, lovey,' she said. 'Playing the old soldier's nothing new in this dump.' She tapped her irons. 'Take my old iron pin. There's some who still ask me to do the can-can before they'll give me the money!'

Peg-Leg made me realise why I got no sympathy, only admiration for a supposed self-inflicted act and envy for having broken my arm, thus earning my passport out of Limbo.

Chapter 16

The Longest Night

I wake and feel the fell of dark, not day.

G. M. Hopkins

Crash! My book fell from my hand, as a pane of glass from the skylight overhead caved in from the force of the gale.

It had taken a month to cut through the circumlocutionary net and I was now just a dawn away from leaving Limbo Hall for ever. I was not spending my last night in bed forty-one, but on a camp-bed in the Casuals Ward.

The Casuals Ward was a great, cold, glass-roofed cavern, adjacent to the main building. Peg-Leg called it the glass-house. That night it was shaking like one. The December gales put sleep out of the question. I had with me a library copy of John O'Hara's *Appointment in Samarra*, intending to read out the storm. It was a prophetic choice. In the preface to his novel, O'Hara quotes some lines from Somerset Maugham's play *Sheppey*, in which a Persian princeling is warned by one of his servants that Death, in the shape of an old crone, has told him she has an appointment with his master on the morrow. The prince bids his servant to saddle his fastest horse. He will ride to Samarra, where Death will not find him. But Death is one jump behind.

Crash! Another pane of glass missed me by a whisker. Better to die the death of a thousand cuts than be attacked by a bunch of female monsters, as had nearly happened earlier that evening in the Regulars Ward.

Rita, the leader of a group of teenage delinquents, had taken it into her head that I was faking a broken arm in order to escape my share of the daily duties. Rita's gang had hauled me out of bed and held me down, while she attempted to unpick the plaster cast from my arm with a flick knife.

My protests brought a settler to the rescue. Not only were the pack deprived of their prey, but Rita was ordered to carry my suitcase to the Casuals Ward, so that I might spend my last night there in relative peace and quiet. Looking up at the already holed skylight, her face a foot away from mine, Rita gibed 'Not exactly the Royal Suite, but you always was one for fresh air!'

She flicked her small pocket torch down the length of the empty ward.

'Looks like you've got it all to yourself tonight. We ought to put up a plaque: "Mrs Armstrong-Jones slept here".' She aimed a vicious kick at my suitcase. 'I'll get you for this, you bloody, stuck-up has been!'

'You'd better be quick,' I said. 'I'm leaving in the morning.'

Crash! The fall of glass was becoming monotonous. The rain was now spreading over my camp bed, so clutching pillow and blankets with my good right hand, I made my way like a lop-sided crab to the bed furthest away from the skylight.

Too dark to read. Too cold anyway. I had left my coat behind on the other bed. Pulling the grey blankets up to my chin, I thought 'Here at least I'll be safe until tomorrow.' But the nagging fear that tomorrow might not come followed me into sleep.

I dreamed I was riding a white horse along the sands in a desperate race against the incoming tide. As I spurred the flagging horse forward, I could smell the blood and sweat from its flanks and taste the salt spray. As my exhausted mount tried to respond to the spur, its rattling breath, louder than the roar of the sea, filled my ears and it fell, dying, beneath me.

Then, suddenly, I was awake. The gale had dropped. The only sound was the pounding of my heart and the dying rattle of the nightmare horse still echoing in my ears.

I reached for a cigarette. Then I heard it again. This time it was no nightmare echo. It was real and came from within the ward.

All lights in the wards are automatically turned out at midnight, but I did not need a light. The sobbing, rattling breath led me straight to the foot of the camp-bed which I had vacated less than an hour ago.

As I turned towards it, my foot touched something hard. I stopped to pick it up. Rita's pocket torch. I flicked it on. Another inch and I would have stepped on a face, or what passed for one. A fountain of blood still bubbled from the mouth, staining the pale hair, which was spread out like a fan on my blood-soaked coat.

The police finally closed their inquiries as unsolved. The fact of finding Rita's torch near the body was not considered conclusive evidence that it was her knife and not falling glass that had struck open the face. But the most damning piece of circumstantial evidence so far as I was concerned was the appearance of the victim. She was exactly my height and colouring and she was wearing my Jaeger coat, which she must have used for a bedcover as I had taken the blanket with me. But it was not enough for a case to be pinned on Rita.

And the victim? Well, she lived. Her name? All I can tell you is that she was a direct descendant of a well-known theatrical family. We went only by numbers at Limbo Hall. And to an ex-Limboite that rule is a code of honour.

Chapter 17

A View from the Wings

It's a long, long while from May to December.
Maxwell Anderson

I was in Girl Friday's office waiting for my discharge card. Like any good dramatic coach she had been preparing me for my next role.

'You never said as much. But one does not have to qualify as a headshrinker to see that you're a writer.'

'Was. Let's get the tense right!'

She smiled over her cigarette. 'Future indicative, surely? If hostel life has done nothing else, it must have provided enough raw material for you to fill at least one book?'

'I don't know. Not yet. Perhaps I'm too raw myself. Too involved. It's still all too real.'

'Twenty-four hours after leaving here you will find it all too unreal. Now's the moment to become uninvolved. Take my tip, before you leave here take a good, hard, long look back.'

The door was flung open by a white-faced settler.

'The girl from the convent, Number Eighteen. She's having a baby in the living-room!'

Girl Friday hurried out after the settler. I lit a cigarette and crossed to the window.

'Take a long, hard look back.'

What did I see? The same view I had seen on that spring

morning when I had become Number Forty-One of Limbo Hall.

At first glimpse this view through a barred window had reminded me of a theatre of the dispossessed. The back-drop was a stone wall. The props were dustbins and garbage. It was almost a Brechtian version of Regent's Park Theatre. I had wondered what unseen, unrecorded dramas had been staged in this bleak auditorium, hidden away in the heart of Limbo. I had imagined too that one woman in her time plays many parts in the ever-changing female cast.

I knew now how wrong I had been. I had learned that one woman during her hostel life has only one part to play. What is more, comedienne, tragedienne, leading lady and walk-on all receive equal billing and, although many make their entrances, few are able to choose the manner or moment of their exit.

I remember the gentle voice of the doctor. 'The worst disease any of my Limbo Hall patients can suffer is just being in here at all.' As I look back, I feel a mixture of anger, fear, doubt and horror, but above all pity and compassion. I can still see Mad Molly, with her wide, staring eyes, standing in front of a painter's easel, but not painting. With a lighted cigarette end she is painstakingly burning holes through the eyes of the figures on the canvas and reciting in a child's voice :

> 'Yesterday, upon a stair,
> I saw a man,
> Who wasn't there.
> He wasn't there again today,
> I wish, I wish, he'd go away !'

And I can see her stabbing the mutilated canvas and screaming 'If he doesn't I'll burn his eyes out ! Yes ! Burn his eyes right out !'

Poor Molly. I was told when I left that the authorities were trying to trace her parents so she could be certified.

I can still see the look in Mrs Brown's eyes as she said 'Faithful'd be better off dead . . . much better off dead.'

I can only imagine the lonely death of the Black Widow.

Few can choose the moment or the manner of their exit. But there is an exception to every rule. Straight up!

I had been talking to Girl Friday when the door was flung open. Marina, the nymph-cherub, rushed in, her breasts peeping out under a flurry of furs. In hot pursuit was a settler, a bra and flimsy panties in her hand.

'Walked right out in the middle of her medical, she did! The doc hadn't even finished 'is examination.'

'Finished!' Marina gave a disdainful giggle. 'He sticks two fingers up. Straight up! Then he starts to play the guitar. "What are you looking for?" I ask. "VD," he says. "Not kicks?" I ask. And he carries on like he hasn't heard. "If you're looking for kicks," I says, "how's that?" And I kicked him good and hard in the bollocks. "If you think I didn't know better than to let a load of clap catch up with me," I says, "you're the one who needs your privates examined." Go on, Forty-one, laugh!'

'You can make me laugh about almost anything, Marina, except when you tell lies about our Doc.'

'Not our Doc, stupid! He's on holiday. Bit of all right, he is. He could have me any day! Told him so, too, I did.'

From the flurry of her fur coat she drew a piece of paper and slapped it down on Girl Friday's desk.

'Put your moniker on that, will you, ducks?'

Girl Friday picked up her pen. 'I don't know that I've ever signed a discharge so gladly.'

Look back . . . Am I looking at myself or the ghost of myself? What about the other Forty-one waiting for the aunt who would never arrive? Would our paths ever cross again?

They did, on Charing Cross Station. An icy wind was blowing across the deserted platform when I saw her, in her usual place, on her usual bench. She looked like a twentieth-century version of Dickens's Miss Havisham. But in place of a decaying wedding gown she was festooned in old newspapers. Her skin, her face, her hands, were as colourless as paper. She was as transparent as glass. The only life was in her eyes. She was staring into space, no longer keeping up the pretence of reading the times of arrivals and departures. But she saw me standing in front of her. Her eyes moved, but with no flicker of recognition; only the silent request 'Please go away. Leave me in peace.'

Tap, tap, tap. Peg-Leg's iron boot still echoes through my nightmares.

> I've changed my abode
> Rather much of late,
> You'll find me at the Park
> Third seat from the gate.

I do not suppose Peg-Leg had ever heard of Roman Emperor August III – an old fraud who enjoyed fooling all the people all of the time. On his death-bed he said 'If I have played my part in the comedy of life, then you must applaud me.'

Show a leg, Peg!

George Orwell, after working as a commis waiter and living in hostels, said there were two things he could never do or enjoy again – have a meal in a good restaurant or give another shilling to charity.

There are two things I can never do or enjoy again. Apart from the fact that my favourite drink is no longer a 'Bloody Mary', I can never again enjoy railway stations. They used to be caverns of adventure, gateways to the world. Now I hurry in and out of them as fast as I can. And if it is after ten at night, mentally I shut my eyes. At night all railway stations are, for me, peopled with living ghosts.

And never again will I look across the Thames, to the other side, the limbo side, without a chill feeling. Even from the comfort of a train, particularly at night, as the train crosses the bridge, if I look out of the carriage window I see only the dark hinterland which lies between hell and Charing Cross. I can feel it even without looking.

Yet there are good memories too. Girl Friday and the doctor, of course; Marina, and the hospital matron who, one night when I had missed the door at one hostel, insisted that I spend what was left of the night in her private room. After bringing me tea, she left me alone, making me promise that for the few hours until dawn I would make believe that the room was my own.

Who else? Star-gazing Louie, a woman whom I only encountered two or three times and with whom I had little in common, except one small coincidence which will haunt me all my life. But it is not an unhappy haunting and the echo of that small coincidence has given me a lasting and warm sense of kinship with those I left behind in limbo.

Louie was a Victorian veteran of the hostel world. When she first entered it there was no Limbo Hall, only the workhouse. Yet, after over half a lifetime spent in Limbo, Louie never lost her inborn yearning for her rightful place in the community, a yearning expressed over and over again not in any tub-thumping tirade or whining about her misfortunes but in three words, three words which I overheard in the darkness of the Regulars Ward.

Lights were out. Louie had just made the door, slightly the worse for wear after her two Friday-night brown ales. At last she got to bed. Silence for a few minutes and then Louie's cracked voice.

'Kitty?'

'Yeah?'

' 'Ave you noticed something about tonight?'

'Yeah, you're tiddly.'

'There aren't any stars.'

'Who cares?'

'I cares! They're my mates, the stars. My mates! Kitty, can I ask you something?'

'Oh, no! Not again!'

'Please, Kitty?'

'Ask a policeman!'

'I did.'

'What did 'e say?'

' "Don't be daft." '

'That's what I say!'

'I know it sounds daft. I just want to know where it flaming is.'

'All right then, for the ninety-ninth time. Mind, you ask me nice and polite like.'

After a deep breath, and then slowly, like a child asking the way to the rainbow's end.

'Beg pardon, I'm sure. But could you please tell me ... Where is Victoria?'

For Louie Victoria was the start of the affluent world across the river, for me it marked the beginning of my journey into limbo.

Once again I felt the warm gentle rain of spring sweep across the darkness of Parliament Square. Again I heard Big Ben striking midnight. One by one all the clocks tolled their melancholy requiem.

Again I found myself staring into that small, strong light.

'Excuse me, officer. But could you please tell me . . . Where is Victoria?'

'Taking a long look back?'

Girl Friday's face was smiling down at me.

'Yes. All the way from May to December.'

Girl Friday handed me a small green form. 'This is yours,' she said. 'And may I say I've never signed a discharge with more certainty of a happy ending.'

'I wonder?'

She held out her hand.

'Goodbye. And good luck, Pamela.'

'Not Forty-one?'

'Queen Anne is dead! You are free to leave when you like. I'm leaving the door open . . .'

And she was gone.

I was alone. The office door stood open. I was free to go. And I could not move. I felt as much a prisoner as on that first night when I had heard the rattle of Bloody Mary's keyring. The little disc, it was that which held me back. I was still wearing it round my neck. It represented an existence when time had stood still, when there was no past, no present, no future – only limbo.

Somewhere, a clock was striking the hour. I crossed to the window and stood looking down. On the darkening courtyard, a tiny bright metal disc, no bigger than a star, mingled with the grey dust. I left Limbo Hall by the back door.

I felt I just had to walk across that silent deserted stage for the last time before I could truly say 'Exit Number Forty-one and this time don't look back !'

I did not.

We met face to face. And now part of me will forever be looking back in memory of the other Forty-one. She was sheltering from the bitter wind, propped up against one of the dustbins. It was like stumbling on a corpse, wrapped from feet to chin in a piece of old sacking. A shroud, by courtesy of British Railways, and bearing the legend 'Lost Property'.

There was no dialogue. Her eyes said it all :

'You're on your way out and so am I . . . I'm ready to make my exit alone. Please go and leave me in peace.'

How could I not obey the silent supplication of my own ghost ?

And so I left her alone on the loneliest stage in the world – the other 'Forty-one'.

> And her . . . That double shee,
> In her dead face,
> Half of yourself shall see . . .

Chapter 18

Afterwards

Now in age, I bud again.
After so many deaths I live and write.

George Herbert

John O'Hara once wrote 'Those who say that time heals all are either kidding themselves or they are too old to remember.'

I shall never grow too old to remember my time in limbo. The anger, frustration and despair are still freshly minted in my mind. Yet, paradoxically, from these bitter memories springs a new joy in life; a joy of the spirit rather than of material things. For instance I can hardly say I have made a complete come-back. My present occupations are the irregular routines of writing, lecturing and broadcasting. But irregular is the operative word and for most of the time I exist dangerously near the bread-line. Yet I have learnt to value the basic fundamentals of living as I have never valued them before. My personal library used to run to hundreds of well-loved volumes, all lost to me now. But next to my own front-door key, my library card has become my most treasured possession.

I live in what is probably the smallest room in Brighton. But it has a balcony and a view of the sea of which I never tire. I realise now my greatest deprivation in limbo was the loss of personal freedom. I could not have lost it more completely had I been in prison and it has taken me several years to regain it fully. Now I celebrate it every hour of my waking day, walking on the downs, looking out at the sea or just turning the key in my own front door. Sometimes the awareness of this gift of re-found freedom is so intense it is like a physical pain and I feel the upsurge of heart that Edna St Vincent Millay must have felt when she wrote 'O World, I cannot hold thee close enough!'

Even as I write hundreds of women are entering the hostel world for the first time. And what of the others, the Peg-Legs, the Louies? Are they still in Limbo Hall? The odds are too heavily stacked against them for the answer to be anything but 'yes'. And what of the few, like myself, who made it back into civilised society? The transition period is not as simple as changing from a third- to a first-class railway carriage. Post-limbo depression is as searing as the hostel doctor warned me it would be. In my nightmares I have always lost my way, as I did that first night trying to find Victoria, and I awake cold with dread.

A nightmare, even one that may recur for the rest of my life, is a bearable legacy. But what happens to the women who have spent years as hostel inmates? Apart from the burden of the mind and the heart of an outcast which require you to grow a new layer of protective skin to face the outside world, there are the practical pitfalls, like the landladies who refuse you a room when they learn you are drawing National Assistance. That happened to me more than once. There are so-called friends who prefer to turn a blind eye and tell you 'If I'd been in the gutter, I wouldn't want to talk about it, let alone write about it.' But I have written about it in order to draw attention to some of the archaic evils that should and can be removed.

Hostels need not be run as if they were prisons. But this means changing the type of woman who works in them. In theory women's hostels should attract, and desperately need, welfare-minded women. Unfortunately, they get throw-outs from other professions – failed policewomen, ex-prison warders, etc. Even in the happiest circumstances women in charge of women can produce tensions. Women in charge of women less fortunate than themselves can and often do result in a hell run by petty dictators. At present most of the officials are semi-professionals in a profession that has not yet produced its own professionals because the qualifications needed are so various and exacting; because the funds are not available either to provide the proper training facilities or to offer adequate monetary rewards to those who graduate; and most important of all, because of the general attitude of our society towards the need for such work and the need for facilities to train the right people to do it. Even in our so-called enlightened era the Welfare State and in particular the Social Services for the under-privileged are something the vast majority prefer not to recognise except as a tug on the sleeve of their conscience. When every so often surveys reveal shocking figures about the number of people living below the poverty line or without homes, most agree that something must be done – but the true facts are quickly forgotten, when some other scandal or tragedy hits the headlines.

Limbo Hall was in my experience the best of hostels. But why is it that standards in the others were so low when it came to sanitation and washing facilities? Why did even Limbo Hall fall down on providing occupations for those prevented from going out in the afternoon by lack of money, lack of a pass, or that hostel disease, fear of the outside world? The answer always comes back to lack of money and adequate staff, and, above all, lack of compassion. Why is identification by number and not name usually the rule? Why is one always locked in and locked out? Why should homeless women lose their rights as free citizens? Their plight asks for compassion, not condemnation. They demand an acknowledgement that their only crimes are heartbreak, desperation, poverty and bad luck. But there are no signs of a change in public attitudes. Homeless women are still looked upon as the lepers of our big cities.

If I were to plead for any one reform, I would plead for the abolition of the most shocking aspect of hostel life, namely that women live their lives on a perpetual see-saw of being locked in or locked out. Without having committed any crime, the hostel dweller is treated mentally and physically like a criminal.

A final note on my nine months of hostel life. Since I was a child, I had always been afraid of counting on tomorrow. Not any more. I now know that life without hope of tomorrow is a negation of life itself. I was one of the fortunate ones. My tomorrowless days were measured in terms of mere months. What about the others, the Peg-Legs, the Black Widows, the

Louie's and the hundreds of women who even now are arriving in limbo for the first time? Unless something is done in those circumlocutionary corridors, what does the future hold for them other than tomorrowless years?